THIS FISH IS LOADED!
THE BOOK OF
SURREAL AND BIZARRE HUMOUR

Edited by

RICHARD GLYN JONES

A CITADEL PRESS BOOK
Published by Carol Publishing Group

A Citadel Press Book
Published by Carol Publishing Group

Editoral Offices
600 Madison Avenue
New York, NY 10022

Sales & Distribution Offices
120 Enterprise Avenue
Secaucus, NJ 07094

First published in Great Britain by Xanadu Publications Ltd
This selection copyright © 1991 by Xanadu Publications Ltd
The copyright notice on page 251 constitute an extension
of this page.

Manufactured in Great Britain

Library of Congress Cataloging-in-Publication Data

This Fish is loaded!: the book of surreal and bizarre humor/
edited by Richard Glyn Jones
        p. cm.
    "A Citadel Press Book."
    ISBN 0-8065-1262-8 (cloth) — ISBN 0-8065-1270-9 (pbk.)
    1. Surrcalism (Literature) — Humor. 2. Surrealism — Humor.
3. Entertainers — Humor. 4. Authors — Humor. I. Jones,
Richard Glyn.
PN6231.S883T45 1991
808.7'91—dc20   91-27712
                                                   CIP

1 2 3 4 5 6 7 8 9 10

CONTENTS

JEAN FERRY

FOREWORD TO SOME OTHER BOOK

S OME DAY, perhaps, these pages may get printed and read.
On the other hand, quite conceivably, the manuscript may
lie for long years silently slumbering in a drawer. The owner
of the chest of drawers may be obliged one day to run away,
leaving the forgotten manuscript behind him. Let's suppose –
why not? – that the chest of drawers is put up for sale and bought
by a wholesale merchant to furnish a maid's bedroom in his new
house. The maid discovers the manuscript and throws it into
the dustbin. The merchant, who can't bear waste – that's how
he made his fortune – sacks the maid, retrieves the manuscript
and sends it to the packing department of his firm. Crumpled,
close-pressed, the papers will serve as padding to line a parcel
being sent to a lonely outpost in the heart of Africa: none of this
is in the least improbable. The package, after months spent in
railway trucks, steamships, hangars, barges, caravans and other
forms of transport, reaches its destination. It has gone to a white
man, who left France some twenty years ago to become the
humble employee of a powerful mining concern, and who now
lingers forgotten in this outpost, which has long since ceased to
function. No other European lives within a radius of a thousand
miles, and this man is surrounded by black men like a white
bean in the middle of a huge sack of black beans. The parcel
has come too late. The man is old. Moreover he had ordered
an ice-making machine and the merchant had by mistake sent
the latest thing in dictaphones. Utterly disgusted, the white
man mechanically uncrumples the manuscript pages that were
wrapped round the virgin cylinders. As he has nothing to do and
is lacking in imagination, he dictates the text once through and
then a second time backwards. And as he is perfectly familiar
with the language of the nearest negro tribe (a debased form

9

of Bomongo) it is in this language that he dictates the first translation of the manuscript. Later on he dies, and is missed by nobody. His hut is overrun and eventually obliterated by the jungle. The manuscript has been long since devoured by red ants.

Meanwhile hostilities have broken out between the tribe of debased Bomongos and a powerful foe. A new hundred years' war begins. After many battles the last of the Bomongos, sole representative henceforward of an extinct race, is obliged to escape into the forest. And there one night, during a tornado, he takes refuge from a pursuing jaguar in the white man's hut – now dim and formless, a bubble of emptiness amidst the close-crowding jungle. The negro discovers the dictaphone, sets it working by accident and hears, in his own tongue, the text of the following pages.

It is for that negro that I am writing.

THE CORPSE CAR

Alphonse Allais

N OT SO LONG ago I had a long talk with the genial head of the *National Federation of Horse Dropping Sweepers (Seine Branch)* and I learnt from him that the livelihood of these good men is becoming highly precarious.

Why?

You all know why.

Because of bicycles and cars!

They are the culprits.

For – and it would be childish to deny it any longer – the horse is not only dying, it is already dead. Henceforth the noblest friend of man is destined to be the petrol-driven vehicle made by Messieurs Dion and Bouton.

True, the Society for the Protection of Animals could recently be heard praising the advent of the car on the grounds that it would relieve their poor nags of such unwanted drudgery. But these otherwise kindly gents of the SPA are too short-sighted to realise that what may be good for animals is bad for long-suffering humanity.

What will the horse dropping sweepers do instead?

What will the spur-makers do?

What will the merchants of riding boots do?

And what will happen to all those industries which may seem far removed from the training and equipping of horses but which will be just as savagely affected by the scourge of this modern invention?

Have you thought, to name only one example, of the effect on undertakers and their horse-drawn hearses? They are, after all, the *only* tradesmen whom we all have to patronise sooner or later. What, I ask you, will be the effect on *them*!

Luckily, it so happens by sheer chance that I am at present

involved in the promotion of a new invention which will solve the problems of all undertakers, because it will replace the horse-drawn funeral hearse *and* the cremation oven at one and the same time.

The necromobile!

(Following the fashion of the day, the inventor of the machine has given it an English name: 'Corpse Car'.)

As you may have perhaps guessed already, the energy necessary to drive the vehicle is derived from the burning of the body of the dear departed. This means that the engine is powered both by steam and gas via a somewhat complicated process. The steam comes from the water content of the late dear one (the human body is, unbelievably, 75% water). The gas is derived from the distillation of the rest of the remains of the poor lamented father (or mother, as the case may be).

My inventor calculates that a dead man of average weight should provide enough fuel to carry at least a dozen funeral guests to a cemetery eight kilometres away.

Which means that at last it will be possible to be simultaneously quick and dead.

THE KUGELMASS EPISODE

Woody Allen

KUGELMASS, a professor of humanities at City College, was unhappily married for the second time. Daphne Kugelmass was an oaf. He also had two dull sons by his first wife, Flo, and was up to his neck in alimony and child support.

'Did I know it would turn out so badly?' Kugelmass whined to his analyst one day. 'Daphne had promise. Who suspected she'd let herself go and swell up like a beach ball? Plus she had a few bucks, which is not in itself a healthy reason to marry a person, but it doesn't hurt, with the kind of operating nut I have. You see my point?'

Kugelmass was bald and as hairy as a bear, but he had soul.

'I need to meet a new woman,' he went on. 'I need to have an affair. I may not look the part, but I'm a man who needs romance. I need softness, I need flirtation. I'm not getting any younger, so before it's too late I want to make love in Venice, trade quips at "21," and exchange coy glances over red wine and candlelight. You see what I'm saying?'

Dr. Mandel shifted in his chair and said, 'An affair will solve nothing. You're so unrealistic. Your problems run much deeper.'

'And also this affair must be discreet,' Kugelmass continued. 'I can't afford a second divorce. Daphne would really sock it to me.'

'Mr. Kugelmass –'

'But it can't be anyone at City College, because Daphne also works there. Not that anyone on the faculty at C.C.N.Y. is any great shakes, but some of those coeds . . .'

'Mr. Kugelmass –'

'Help me. I had a dream last night. I was skipping through

a meadow holding a picnic basket and the basket was marked "Options." And then I saw there was a hole in the basket.'

'Mr. Kugelmass, the worst thing you could do is act out. You must simply express your feelings here, and together we'll analyze them. You have been in treatment long enough to know there is no overnight cure. After all, I'm an analyst, not a magician.'

'Then perhaps what I need is a magician,' Kugelmass said, rising from his chair. And with that he terminated his therapy.

A couple of weeks later, while Kugelmass and Daphne were moping around in their apartment one night like two pieces of old furniture, the phone rang.

'I'll get it,' Kugelmass said. 'Hello.'

'Kugelmass?' a voice said. 'Kugelmass, this is Persky.'

'Who?'

'Persky. Or should I say The Great Persky?'

'Pardon me?'

'I hear you're looking all over town for a magician to bring a little exotica into your life? Yes or no?'

'Sh-h-h,' Kugelmass whispered. 'Don't hang up. Where are you calling from, Persky?'

Early the following afternoon, Kugelmass climbed three flights of stairs in a broken-down apartment house in the Bushwick section of Brooklyn. Peering through the darkness of the hall, he found the door he was looking for and pressed the bell. I'm going to regret this, he thought to himself.

Seconds later, he was greeted by a short, thin, waxy-looking man.

'*You're* Persky the Great?' Kugelmass said.

'The Great Persky. You want a tea?'

'No, I want romance. I want music. I want love and beauty.'

'But not tea, eh? Amazing. O.K., sit down.'

Persky went to the back of the room, and Kugelmass heard the sounds of boxes and furniture being moved around. Persky reappeared, pushing before him a large object on squeaky roller-skate wheels. He removed some old silk handkerchiefs that were lying on its top and blew away a bit of dust. It was a cheap-looking Chinese cabinet, badly lacquered.

'Persky,' Kugelmass said, 'what's your scam?'

'Pay attention,' Persky said. 'This is some beautiful effect. I developed it for a Knights of Pythias date last year, but the booking fell through. Get into the cabinet.'

'Why, so you can stick it full of swords or something?'

'You see any swords?'

Kugelmass made a face and, grunting, climbed into the cabinet. He couldn't help noticing a couple of ugly rhinestones glued onto the raw plywood just in front of his face. 'If this is a joke,' he said.

'Some joke. Now, here's the point. If I throw any novel into this cabinet with you, shut the doors, and tap it three times, you will find yourself projected into that book.'

Kugelmass made a grimace of disbelief.

'It's the emess,' Persky said. 'My hand to God. Not just a novel, either. A short story, a play, a poem. You can meet any of the women created by the world's best writers. Whoever you dreamed of. You could carry on all you like with a real winner. Then when you've had enough you give a yell, and I'll see you're back here in a split second.'

'Persky, are you some kind of outpatient?'

'I'm telling you it's on the level,' Persky said.

Kugelmass remained skeptical. 'What are you telling me – that this cheesy homemade box can take me on a ride like you're describing?'

'For a double sawbuck.'

Kugelmass reached for his wallet. 'I'll believe this when I see it,' he said.

Persky tucked the bills in his pants pocket and turned toward his bookcase. 'So who do you want to meet? Sister Carrie? Hester Prynne? Ophelia? Maybe someone by Saul Bellow? Hey, what about Temple Drake? Although for a man your age she'd be a workout.'

'French. I want to have an affair with a French lover.'

'Nana?'

'I don't want to have to pay for it.'

'What about Natasha in *War and Peace?*'

'I said French. I know! What about Emma Bovary? That sounds to me perfect.'

'You got it, Kugelmass. Give me a holler when you've had enough.' Persky tossed in a paperback copy of Flaubert's novel.

'You sure this is safe?' Kugelmass asked as Persky began shutting the cabinet doors.

'Safe. Is anything safe in this crazy world?' Persky rapped three times on the cabinet and then flung open the doors.

Kugelmass was gone. At the same moment, he appeared in the bedroom of Charles and Emma Bovary's house at Yonville. Before him was a beautiful woman, standing alone with her back turned to him as she folded some linen. I can't believe this, thought Kugelmass, staring at the doctor's ravishing wife. This is uncanny. I'm here. It's her.

Emma turned in surprise. 'Goodness, you startled me,' she said. 'Who are you?' She spoke in the same fine English translation as the paperback.

It's simply devastating, he thought. Then, realizing that it was he whom she had addressed, he said, 'Excuse me. I'm Sidney Kugelmass. I'm from City College. A professor of humanities. C.C.N.Y.? Uptown. I – oh, boy!'

Emma Bovary smiled flirtatiously and said, 'Would you like a drink? A glass of wine, perhaps?'

She is beautiful, Kugelmass thought. What a contrast with the troglodyte who shared his bed! He felt a sudden impulse to take this vision into his arms and tell her she was the kind of woman he had dreamed of all his life.

'Yes, some wine,' he said hoarsely. 'White. No, red. No, white. Make it white.'

'Charles is out for the day,' Emma said, her voice full of playful implications.

After the wine, they went for a stroll in the lovely French

countryside. 'I've always dreamed that some mysterious stranger would appear and rescue me from the monotony of this crass rural existence,' Emma said, clasping his hand. They passed a small church. 'I love what you have on,' she murmured. 'I've never seen anything like it around here. It's so . . . so modern.'

'It's called a leisure suit,' he said romantically. 'It was marked down.' Suddenly he kissed her. For the next hour they reclined under a tree and whispered together and told each other deeply meaningful things with their eyes. Then Kugelmass sat up. He had just remembered he had to meet Daphne at Bloomingdale's. 'I must go,' he told her. 'But don't worry, I'll be back.'

'I hope so,' Emma said.

He embraced her passionately, and the two walked back to the house. He held Emma's face cupped in his palms, kissed her again, and yelled, 'O.K., Persky! I got to be at Bloomingdale's by three-thirty.'

There was an audible pop, and Kugelmass was back in Brooklyn.

'So? Did I lie?' Persky asked triumphantly.

'Look, Persky, I'm right now late to meet the ball and chain at Lexington Avenue, but when can I go again? Tomorrow?'

'My pleasure. Just bring a twenty. And don't mention this to anybody.'

'Yeah. I'm going to call Rupert Murdoch.'

Kugelmass hailed a cab and sped off to the city. His heart danced on point. I am in love, he thought, I am the possessor of a wonderful secret. What he didn't realize was that at this moment students in various classrooms across the country were saying to their teachers, 'Who is this character on page 100? A bald Jew is kissing Madame Bovary?' A teacher in Sioux Falls, South Dakota, sighed and thought, Jesus, these kids, with their pot and acid. What goes through their minds!

Daphne Kugelmass was in the bathroom-accessories department at Bloomingdale's when Kugelmass arrived breathlessly. 'Where've you been?' she snapped. 'It's four-thirty.'

'I got held up in traffic,' Kugelmass said.

Kugelmass visited Persky the next day, and in a few minutes was again passed magically to Yonville. Emma couldn't hide her excitement at seeing him. The two spent hours together, laughing and talking about their different backgrounds. Before Kugelmass left, they made love. 'My God, I'm doing it with Madame Bovary!' Kugelmass whispered to himself. 'Me, who failed freshman English.'

As the months passed, Kugelmass saw Persky many times and developed a close and passionate relationship with Emma Bovary. 'Make sure and always get me into the book before page 120,' Kugelmass said to the magician one day. 'I always have to meet her before she hooks up with this Rodolphe character.'

'Why?' Persky asked. 'You can't beat his time?'

'Beat his time. He's landed gentry. Those guys have nothing better to do than flirt and ride horses. To me, he's one of those faces you see in the pages of *Women's Wear Daily*. With the Helmut Berger hairdo. But to her he's hot stuff.'

'And her husband suspects nothing?'

'He's out of his depth. He's a lacklustre little paramedic who's thrown in his lot with a jitterbug. He's ready to go to sleep by ten, and she's putting on her dancing shoes. Oh, well . . . See you later.'

And once again Kugelmass entered the cabinet and passed instantly to the Bovary estate at Yonville. 'How you doing cupcake?' he said to Emma.

'Oh, Kugelmass,' Emma sighed. 'What I have to put up with. Last night at dinner, Mr. Personality dropped off to sleep in the middle of the dessert course. I'm pouring my heart out about Maxim's and the ballet, and out of the blue I hear snoring.'

'It's O.K., darling. I'm here now.' Kugelmass said, embracing her. I've earned this, he thought, smelling Emma's French perfume and burying his nose in her hair. I've suffered enough. I've paid enough analysts. I've searched till I'm weary. She's young and nubile, and I'm here a few pages after Leon and just before Rodolphe. By showing up during the correct chapters, I've got the situation knocked.

Emma, to be sure, was just as happy as Kugelmass. She had been starved for excitement, and his tales of Broadway life, of fast cars and Hollywood and TV stars, enthralled the young French beauty.

'Tell me again about O.J. Simpson,' she implored that evening, as she and Kugelmass strolled past Abbé Bournisien's church.

'What can I say? The man is great. He sets all kinds of rushing records. Such moves. They can't touch him.'

'And the Academy Awards?' Emma said wistfully. 'I'd give anything to win one.'

'First you've got to be nominated.'

'I know. You explained it. But I'm convinced I can act. Of course, I'd want to take a class or two. With Strasberg maybe. Then, if I had the right agent –'

'We'll see, we'll see. I'll speak to Persky.'

That night, safely returned to Persky's flat, Kugelmass brought up the idea of having Emma visit him in the big city.

'Let me think about it,' Persky said. 'Maybe I could work it. Stranger things have happened.' Of course, neither of them could think of one.

'Where the hell do you go all the time?' Daphne Kugelmass barked at her husband as he returned home late that evening. 'You got a chippie stashed somewhere?'

'Yeah, sure, I'm just the type,' Kugelmass said wearily. 'I was with Leonard Popkin. We were discussing Socialist agriculture in Poland. You know Popkin. He's a freak on the subject.'

'Well, you've been very odd lately,' Daphne said. 'Distant.

Just don't forget about my father's birthday. On Saturday?'

'Oh, sure, sure,' Kugelmass said, heading for the bathroom.

'My whole family will be there. We can see the twins. And Cousin Hamish. You should be more polite to Cousin Hamish – he likes you.'

'Right, the twins,' Kugelmass said, closing the bathroom door and shutting out the sound of his wife's voice. He leaned against it and took a deep breath. In a few hours he told himself, he would be back in Yonville again, with his beloved. And this time, if all went well, he would bring Emma back with him.

At three-fifteen the following afternoon, Persky worked his wizardry again. The two spent a few hours at Yonville with Binet and then remounted the Bovary carriage. Following Persky's instructions, they held each other tightly, closed their eyes, and counted to ten. When they opened them, the carriage was just drawing up at the side door of the Plaza Hotel, where Kugelmass had optimistically reserved a suite earlier in the day.

'I love it! It's everything I dreamed it would be,' Emma said as she swirled joyously around the bedroom, surveying the city from their window. 'There's F.A.O. Schwarz. And there's Central Park, and the Sherry is which one? Oh, there – I see. It's too divine.'

On the bed there were boxes from Halston and Saint Laurent. Emma unwrapped a package and held up a pair of black velvet pants against her perfect body.

'The slacks suit is by Ralph Lauren,' Kugelmass said. 'You'll look like a million bucks in it. Come on, sugar, give us a kiss.'

'I've never been so happy!' Emma squealed as she stood before the mirror. 'Let's go out on the town. I want to see *Chorus Line* and the Guggenheim and this Jack Nicholson character you always talk about. Are any of his flicks showing?'

'I cannot get my mind around this,' a Stanford professor said. 'First a strange character named Kugelmass, and now she's gone from the book. Well, I guess the mark of a classic is that you can reread it a thousand times and always find something new.'

The lovers passed a blissful weekend. Kugelmass had told Daphne he would be away at a symposium in Boston and would return Monday. Savoring each moment, he and Emma went to the movies, had dinner in Chinatown, passed two hours at a discothèque, and went to bed with a TV movie. They slept till noon on Sunday, visited SoHo, and ogled celebrities at Elaine's. They had caviar and champagne in their suite on Sunday night and talked until dawn. That morning, in the cab taking them to Persky's apartment, Kugelmass thought, it was hectic, but worth it. I can't bring her here too often, but now and then it will be a charming contrast with Yonville.

At Persky's Emma climbed into the cabinet, arranged her new boxes of clothes neatly around her, and kissed Kugelmass fondly. 'My place next time,' she said with a wink. Persky rapped three times on the cabinet. Nothing happened.

'Hmm,' Persky said, scratching his head. He rapped again, but still no magic. 'Something must be wrong,' he mumbled.

'Persky, you're joking!' Kugelmass cried. 'How can it not work?'

'Relax, relax. Are your still in the box, Emma?'

'Yes.'

Persky rapped again – harder this time.

'I'm still here, Persky.'

'I know, darling. Sit tight.'

'Persky, we *have* to get her back,' Kugelmass whispered. 'I'm a married man, and I have a class in three hours. I'm not prepared for anything more than a cautious affair at this point.'

'I can't understand it,' Persky muttered. 'It's such a reliable little trick.'

But he could do nothing. 'It's going to take a little while,' he said to Kugelmass. 'I'm going to have to strip it down. I'll call you later.'

Kugelmass bundled Emma into a cab and took her back to

the Plaza. He barely made it to his class on time. He was on the phone all day, to Persky and to his mistress. The magician told him it might be several days before he got to the bottom of the trouble.

'How was the symposium?' Daphne asked him that night.

'Fine, fine,' he said, lighting the filter end of a cigarette.

'What's wrong? You're as tense as a cat.'

'Me? Ha, that's a laugh. I'm as calm as a summer night. I'm just going to take a walk.' He eased out the door, hailed a cab, and flew to the Plaza.

'This is no good,' Emma said. 'Charles will miss me.'

'Bear with me sugar,' Kugelmass said. He was pale and sweaty. He kissed her again, raced to the elevators, yelled at Persky over a pay phone in the Plaza lobby, and just made it home before midnight.

'According to Popkin, barley prices in Kraków have not been this stable since 1971,' he said to Daphne, and smiled wanly as he climbed into bed.

The whole week went like that.

On Friday night, Kugelmass told Daphne there was another symposium he had to catch, this one in Syracuse. He hurried back to the Plaza, but the second weekend there was nothing like the first. 'Get me back into the novel or marry me,' Emma told Kugelmass. 'Meanwhile, I want to get a job or go to class, because watching TV all day is the pits.'

'Fine. We can use the money,' Kugelmass said. 'You consume twice your weight in room service.'

'I met an Off Broadway producer in Central Park yesterday, and he told me I might be right for a project he's doing,' Emma said.

'Who is this clown?' Kugelmass asked.

'He's not a clown. He's sensitive and kind and cute. His name's Jeff Something-or-Other, and he's up for a Tony.'

Later that afternoon, Kugelmass showed up at Persky's drunk.

'Relax,' Persky told him. 'You'll get a coronary.'

'Relax.' The man says relax. I've got a fictional character stashed in a hotel room, and I think my wife is having me tailed by a private shamus.'

'O.K., O.K. We know there's a problem.' Persky crawled under the cabinet and started banging on something with a large wrench.

'I'm like a wild animal,' Kugelmass went on. 'I'm sneaking around town, and Emma and I have had it up to here with each other. Not to mention a hotel tab that reads like a defense budget.'

'So what should I do? This is the world of magic,' Persky said. 'It's all nuance.'

'Nuance, my foot. I'm pouring Dom Pérignon and black eggs into this little mouse, plus her wardrobe, plus she's enrolled at the Neighborhood Playhouse and suddenly needs professional photos. Also, Persky, Professor Faivish Kopkind, who teaches Comp Lit and who has always been jealous of me, has identified me as the sporadically appearing character in the Flaubert book. He's threatened to go to Daphne. I see ruin and alimony; jail. For adultery with Madame Bovary, my wife will reduce me to beggary.'

'What do you want me to say? I'm working on it night and day. As far as your personal anxiety goes, that I can't help you with. I'm a magician, not an analyst.'

By Sunday afternoon, Emma had locked herself in the bathroom and refused to respond to Kugelmass's entreaties. Kugelmass stared out the window at the Wollman Rink and contemplated suicide. Too bad this is a low floor, he thought, or I'd do it right now. Maybe if I ran away to Europe and started life over . . . Maybe I could sell the *International Herald Tribune*, like those young girls used to.

The phone rang. Kugelmass lifted it to his ear mechanically.

'Bring her over,' Persky said. 'I think I got the bugs out of it.'

Kugelmass's heart leaped. 'You're serious?' he said. 'You got it licked?'

'It was something in the transmission. Go figure.'

'Persky, you're a genius. We'll be there in a minute. Less than a minute.'

Again the lovers hurried to the magician's apartment, and again Emma Bovary climbed into the cabinet with her boxes. This time there was no kiss. Persky shut the doors, took a deep breath, and tapped the box three times. There was the reassuring popping noise; and when Persky peered inside, the box was empty. Madame Bovary was back in her novel. Kugelmass heaved a great sigh of relief and pumped the magician's hand.

'It's over,' he said. 'I learned my lesson. I'll never cheat again, I swear it.' He pumped Persky's hand again and made a mental note to send him a necktie.

Three weeks later, at the end of a beautiful spring afternoon, Persky answered his doorbell. It was Kugelmass, with a sheepish expression on his face.

'O.K., Kugelmass,' the magician said. 'Where to this time?'

'It's just this once,' Kugelmass said. 'The weather is so lovely, and I'm not getting any younger. Listen, you've read *Portnoy's Complaint*? Remember The Monkey?'

'The price is now twenty-five dollars, because the cost of living is up, but I'll start you off with one freebie, due to all the trouble I caused you.'

'You're good people,' Kugelmass said, combing his few remaining hairs as he climbed into the cabinet again. 'This'll work all right?'

'I hope. But I haven't tried it much since all that unpleasantness.'

'Sex and romance,' Kugelmass said from inside the box. 'What we go through for a pretty face.'

Persky tossed in a copy of *Portnoy's Complaint* and rapped three times on the box. This time, instead of a popping noise there was a dull explosion, followed by a series of crackling noises and a shower of sparks. Persky leaped back, was seized by a heart attack, and dropped dead. The cabinet burst into flames, and eventually the entire house burned down.

Kugelmass, unaware of this catastrophe, had his own problems. He had not been thrust into *Portnoy's Complaint*, or into any other novel, for that matter. He had been projected into an old textbook, *Remedial Spanish*, and was running for his life over a barren, rocky terrain as the word *tener* ('to have') – a large and hairy irregular verb – raced after him on its spindly legs.

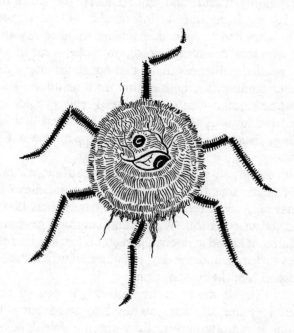

THE DISAPPEARANCE OF HONORÉ SUBRAC

Guillaume Apollinaire

I N SPITE OF THE most minute investigations, the police have never been able to throw any light on the mystery of the disappearance of Honoré Subrac.

He was my friend, and since I knew the truth about his case, I made it my duty to inform the judicial authorities of exactly what had happened. After listening to my story, the judge who took down my deposition spoke to me in a voice of such appalled politeness that I had not the slightest difficulty in understanding that he took me for a madman. I told him so, and he became even more polite. Finally, standing up, he pushed me towards the door, where I noticed his clerk was standing, fists clenched, ready to deal with me if I became violent.

I did not insist. The case of Honoré Subrac is, in fact, so extraordinary that the truth itself seems unbelievable. You may have learned from stories in the newspapers that Subrac passed for an eccentric. Winter and summer, he wore as his only garment an old greatcoat, and on his feet a pair of slippers. He was very rich, and one day, because his outfit astonished me so, I asked him the reason for it:

'It is to enable me to undress quickly in case of need,' he answered. 'After all, one gets used to going out with very little on. It is quite easy to do without a shirt, socks and a hat. I have lived like this since the age of twenty-five, and I have never been ill.'

These words, far from being enlightening, only served to sharpen my curiosity.

I thought to myself: 'Why on earth does Honoré Subrac have to get undressed in such a hurry?'

And I may say that I conjured up a great many suppositions.

One night when I was going home – it might have been one o'clock or a quarter past – I heard my name spoken in a low voice. It seemed to come straight from a wall near which I was passing. I stopped, disagreeably surprised.

'Is there anyone else still on the road? It's me,' the voice continued, 'Honoré Subrac.'

'But where are you?' I cried, looking all round me without being able to make out where my friend was hiding.

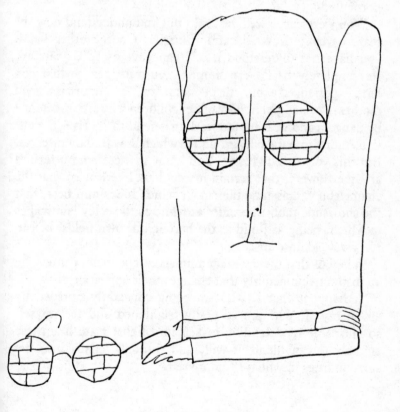

All I could find was his famous greatcoat, lying on the pavement, and beside it his equally famous slippers.

'Here obviously is an occasion,' I thought, 'when necessity compelled Honoré Subrac to get undressed in the twinkling of an eye. At last, I am going to reveal his great mystery.'

And I said out loud:

'The street is deserted, my dear friend. You may come out.'

Honoré Subrac somehow suddenly emerged from the wall at a place where I had not noticed him. He was stark naked, and before doing anything else, he picked up his greatcoat, put it on, and buttoned it up as fast as he could. He then put on his slippers, and accompanied me to my door, talking quite normally:

'You were surprised!' he said, 'but you understand now the reason why I dress so extraordinarily. On the other hand, you have not understood how I can have escaped your eye so completely. It is very simple. You must realize that you have experienced a mimetic phenomenon . . . Nature is a good mother. She has given those of her children who are threatened by dangers and who are too weak to defend themselves the gift of blending into the background in which they find themselves. But this you already know. You know that certain butterflies are like flowers, that certain insects look like leaves, that the chameleon can assume the colour which hides him best, that the snowshoe rabbit becomes as white as those icy landscapes in which, being as timid as the hare in our own fields, he can run away, almost unseen.

'It is thus that these weaker animals escape their enemies; by an instinctive ingenuity that changes their appearance.

'It happens that I, who am being constantly pursued by an enemy; I, who am so easily frightened and feel myself so incapable of defending myself in a fight; I am like these animals. I can blend at will, and through terror, into the surroundings in which I find myself.

'I used this instinctive faculty for the first time some years ago now. I was twenty years old, and women generally found me pleasing and handsome. One of them, who was married, had such a taste for me that I could resist no longer. The liaison proved disastrous! One night, I was with my mistress. Her husband was supposed to be away from the house for several days. We were naked as the gods, when the door flew open, and her husband appeared, revolver in hand. My terror was indescribable, and I had but one desire, coward that I was, and still am – to disappear utterly. Leaning for support against a wall, I wished desperately that I might blend into it. And the unexpected immediately happened. I became the colour of the wallpaper, and my limbs flattened themselves of their own accord in some inconceivable manner, until it seemed to me that I was one with the wall, and furthermore, that no one could see me. It was true. The husband searched for me, intent on killing me. He had seen me, and it was impossible that I should have escaped. He became mad with rage and, turning on his wife, he killed her savagely, firing six shots into her head. He then left, weeping in despair. After he had gone, instinctively, my body returned to its normal shape and natural colour. I dressed myself, and managed to leave the house before anyone had seen me. This blessed faculty, a branch of animal mimetism, I have kept ever since. Not having killed me, the husband has devoted his life to accomplishing this task. He has followed me all over the world for several years, and I thought I had managed to escape him by coming to live in Paris. But I saw him an instant before you arrived. My teeth chattered with fright. I only just had time to get undressed and melt into the wall. He passed right beside me, stopping for a moment to glance curiously at my greatcoat and slippers, which lay abandoned on the pavement. Now you see how right I am to dress in this way. My mimetic faculty would not exert itself were I dressed like everyone else. I would not be able to undress quickly enough to escape my executioner, because it is above all essential for me to be naked, so that my clothes, flattened against the wall, do not render my protective disappearance useless.'

I congratulated Subrac on possessing a faculty of which I had had proof, and which I envied him . . .

For the next few days I thought of nothing else, and I surprised myself at every turn bending my will towards modifying my own shape and colour. I endeavoured to change myself into a bus, into the Eiffel Tower, into the winner of the first prize in a lottery, and into an Academician. My efforts were in vain. I was not up to it. My willpower was not strong enough; also, I lacked that holy terror, and the formidable danger, which had roused Honoré Subrac's instinct . . .

I had not seen him for some time when, one day, he arrived at my house, scared almost out of his life:

'This man, my enemy,' he told me, 'is watching me everywhere I go. I have managed to escape him three times by exercising my faculty, but I am afraid, I am afraid, my dear friend.'

I noticed that he had grown thinner, but was careful not to tell him this.

'There is only one thing for you to do,' I declared. 'In order to escape this pitiless character, you must go away! Hide in some village! Leave me in charge of your affairs, and go at once to the nearest railway station.'

He wrung my hand, saying:

'Come with me then, I beg you. I am afraid!'

In the street, we walked in silence, with Honoré Subrac constantly turning his head around with an air of extreme anxiety. Suddenly, he gave a yell and broke into a run, shedding his greatcoat and slippers as he went. I saw a man running towards us from behind, and tried to stop him, but he escaped me. He had a revolver in his hand which he aimed at Honoré Subrac. The latter had just reached the wall of the barracks when he disappeared, as if by magic.

The man with the revolver stopped, stupefied, with a cry of rage; then, as if to avenge himself on the wall which seemed to have robbed him of his victim at the last moment, he fired his revolver at the very spot where Honoré Subrac had vanished, then ran off . . .

The police came and dispersed the crowd that had begun to assemble. I called my friend, but he did not reply.

I felt the wall. *It was still warm*, and I noticed that of the six revolver shots, three had hit the wall at the height of a man's heart, while the other three had shattered the plaster higher up, at a point where I seemed to be able to distinguish, vaguely, the outline of a face.

BRAIN DAMAGE

Donald Barthelme

IN THE FIRST garbage dump I found a book describing a rich new life of achievement, prosperity, and happiness. A rich new life of achievement, prosperity, and happiness could not be achieved alone, the book said. It must be achieved with the aid of spirit teachers. At long last a way had been found to reach the spirit world. Once the secret was learned, spirit teachers would assist you through the amazing phenomenon known as ESP. My spirit teachers wanted to help me, the book said. As soon as I contacted them, they would do everything in their power to grant my desires. An example, on page 117: A middle-aged woman was being robbed, but as the thief was taking her purse, a flash of blue light like a tiny lightning bolt knocked his gun out of his hands and he fled in terror. That was just the beginning, the book said. One could learn how to eliminate hostility from the hearts of others.

We thought about the blue flowers. Different people had different ideas about them. Henry wanted to 'turn them on.' We brought wires and plugs and a screwdriver, and wired the green ends of the flowers (the bottom part, where they had been cut) to the electrical wire. We were sort of afraid to plug them in, though – afraid of all that electricity pushing its way up the green stalks of the flowers, flooding the leaves, and finally touching the petals, the blue part, where the blueness of the flowers resided, along with white, and a little yellow. 'What kind of current is this, that we are possibly going to plug the flowers into?' Gregory asked. It seemed to be alternating current rather than direct current. That was what we all thought, because most of the houses in this part of the country were built in compliance with building codes that required AC.

In fact, you don't find much DC around any more, because in the early days of electricity, many people were killed by it.

'Well, plug them in,' Grace said. Because she wanted to see the flowers light up, or collapse, or do whatever they were going to do, when they were plugged in.

The humanist position is not to plug in the flowers – to let them alone. Humanists believe in letting everything alone to be what it is, insofar as possible. The new electric awareness, however, requires that the flowers be plugged in, right away. Toynbee's notions of challenge and response are also, perhaps, apposite. My own idea about whether or not to plug in the flowers is somewhere between these ideas, in that gray area where nothing is done, really, but you vacillate for a while, thinking about it. The blue of the flowers is extremely handsome against the gray of that area.

CROWD NOISES

MURMURING

MURMURING

YAWNING

A great waiter died, and all of the other waiters were saddened. At the restaurant, sadness was expressed. Black napkins were draped over black arms. Black tablecloths were distributed. Several nearby streets were painted black – those leading to

the establishment in which Guignol had placed his plates with legendary tact. Guignol's medals (for like a great beer he had been decorated many times, at international exhibitions in Paris, Brussels, Rio de Janeiro) were turned over to his mistress, La Lupe. The body was poached in white wine, stock, olive oil, vinegar, aromatic vegetables, herbs, garlic, and slices of lemon for twenty-four hours and displayed *en Aspic* on a bed of lettuce leaves. Hundreds of famous triflers appeared to pay their last respects. Guignol's colleagues recalled with pleasure the master's most notable eccentricity. Having coolly persuaded some innocent to select a thirty-dollar bottle of wine, he never failed to lean forward conspiratorially and whisper in his victim's ear, 'Cuts the grease.'

RETCHING

FAINTING

DISMAL BEHAVIOR
TENDERING OF EXCUSES

A dream: I am looking at a ship, an ocean-going vessel the size of the Michelangelo. But unlike the Michelangelo this ship is not painted a dazzling white; it is caked with rust. And it is not in the water. The whole immense bulk of it sits on dry land. Furthermore it is loaded with high explosives which may go off at any moment. My task is to push the ship through a narrow mountain pass whose cliffs rush forward threateningly. An experience: I was crossing the street in the rain holding an umbrella. On the other side of the street an older woman was motioning to me. Come here, come here! I indicated that I didn't want to come there, wasn't interested, had other things to do. But she continued to make motions, to insist. Finally I went over to her. 'Look down there,' she said pointing to the gutter full of water, 'there's a penny. Don't you want to pick it up?'

I worked for newspapers. I worked for newspapers at a time when I was not competent to do so. I reported inaccurately. I failed to get all the facts. I misspelled names. I garbled figures. I wasted copy paper. I pretended I knew things I did not know. I pretended to understand things beyond my understanding. I oversimplified. I was superior to things I was inferior to. I misinterpreted things that took place before me. I over- and underinterpreted what took place before me. I suppressed news the management wanted suppressed. I invented news the management wanted invented. I faked stories. I failed to discover the truth. I colored the truth with fancy. I had no respect for the truth. I failed to heed the adage: you shall know the truth and the truth shall make you free. I put lies in the paper. I put private jokes in the paper. I wrote headlines

35

containing *double entendres*. I wrote stories while drunk. I abused copy boys. I curried favor with advertisers. I accepted gifts from interested parties. I was servile with superiors. I was harsh with people who called on the telephone seeking information. I gloated over police photographs of sex crimes. I touched type when the makeups weren't looking. I took copy pencils home. I voted with management in Guild elections.

RHYTHMIC HANDCLAPPING
SLEEPING
WHAT RECOURSE?

The Wapituil are like us to an extraordinary degree. They have a kinship system which is very similar to our kinship system. They

address each other as 'Mister,' 'Mistress,' and 'Miss.' They wear clothes which look very much like our clothes. They have a Fifth Avenue which divides their territory into east and west. They have a Chock Full o'Nuts and a Chevrolet, one of each.

They have a Museum of Modern Art and a telephone and a Martini, one of each. The Martini and the telephone are kept in the Museum of Modern Art. In fact they have everything that we have, but only one of each thing.

We found that they lose interest very quickly. For instance they are fully industrialized, but they don't seem interested in taking advantage of it. After the steel mill produced the ingot, it was shut down. They can conceptualize but they don't follow through. For instance, their week has seven days – Monday, Monday, Monday, Monday, Monday, Monday, and Monday. They have one disease, mononucleosis. The sex life of a Wapituil consists of a single experience, which he thinks about for a long time.

Behavior of the waiters: The first waiter gave a twenty-cent tip to the second waiter. The second waiter looked down at the two dimes in his hand and then up at the first waiter. Looks of disgust were exchanged. The third waiter put a dollar bill on a plate and handed it to the fourth waiter. The fourth waiter took the dollar bill and stuffed it into his pocket. Then the fourth waiter took six quarters from another pocket and made a neat little stack of quarters next to the elbow of the fifth waiter, who was sitting at a rear table, writing on a little pad. The fifth waiter gave the captain a five-dollar bill which the captain slipped into a pocket in the tail of his tailcoat. The sixth waiter handed the seventh waiter a small envelope

WRITHING

HOWLING

MOANS

WHAT RECOURSE?

RHYTHMIC HANDCLAPPING

SHOUTING

SEXUAL ACTIVITY

CONSUMPTION OF FOOD

containing two ten-dollar bills. The seventh waiter put a small leather bag containing twelve louis d'or into the bosom of the wife of the eighth waiter. The ninth waiter offered a $50 War Bond to the tenth waiter, who was carrying a crystal casket of carbuncles to the chef.

The cup fell from nerveless fingers . . .

The china cup big as an AFB fell from tiny white nerveless fingers no bigger than hairs . . .

'Sit down. I am your spiritual adviser. Sit down and have a cup of tea with me. See, there is the chair. There is the cup. The tea boy will bring the tea shortly. When the tea boy brings the tea, you may pour some of it into your cup. That cup there, on the table.'

'Thank you. This is quite a nice University you have here. A University constructed entirely of three mile-high sponges!'

'Yes it is rather remarkable.'

'What is that very large body with hundreds and hundreds of legs moving across the horizon from left to right in a steady, carefully considered line?'

'That is the tenured faculty crossing to the other shore on the plane of the feasible.'

'And this tentacle here of the Underwater Life Sciences Department . . .'

'That is not a tentacle but the Department itself. Devouring a whole cooked chicken furnished by the Department of Romantic Poultry.'

'And those running men?'

'Those are the runners.'

'What are they running from?'

'They're not running from, they're running toward. Trained in the Department of Great Expectations.'

'Is that my Department?'

'Do you blush easily?'

The elevator girls were standing very close together. One girl put a candy bar into another girl's mouth and then another girl put a hamburger into another girl's mouth. Another girl put a Kodak Instamatic camera to her eye and took a picture of another girl and another girl patted another girl on the shapely caudal area. Giant aircraft passed in the sky, their passengers bent over with their heads between their knees, in pillows. The Mother Superior spoke. 'No, dear friend, it cannot be. It is not that we don't believe that your renunciation of the world is real. We believe it is real. But you look like the kind who is overly susceptible to Nun's Melancholy, which is one of our big problems here. Therefore full membership is impossible. We will send the monks to you, at the end. The monks sing well, too. We will send the monks to you, for your final agony.' I turned away. This wasn't what I wanted to hear. I went out into the garage and told Bill an interesting story which wasn't true. Some people feel you should tell the truth, but those people are impious and wrong, and if you listen to what they say, you will be tragically unhappy all your life.

TO WHAT END?

IN WHOSE NAME?

WHAT RECOURSE?

Oh there's brain damage in the east, and brain damage in the west, and upstairs there's brain damage, and downstairs there's brain damage, and in my lady's parlor – brain damage. Brain damage is widespread. Apollinaire was a victim of brain damage – you remember the photograph, the bandage on his head, and the poems . . . Bonnie and Clyde suffered from brain damage in the last four minutes of the picture. There's brain damage on the horizon, a great big blubbery cloud of it coming this way –

And you can hide under the bed but brain damage is under the bed, and you can hide in the universities but they are the very seat and soul of brain damage – Brain damage caused by bears who put your head in their foaming jaws while you are singing 'Masters of War' . . . Brain damage caused by the sleeping revolution which no one can wake up . . . Brain damage caused by art. I could describe it better if I weren't afflicted with it . . .

This is the country of brain damage, this is the map of brain damage, these are the rivers of brain damage, and see, those lighted-up places are the airports of brain damage, where the damaged pilots land the big, damaged ships.

The Immaculate Conception triggered a lot of brain damage at one time, but no longer does so. A team of Lippizaners has just published an autobiography. Is that any reason to accuse them of you-know-what? And I saw a girl walking down the street, she was singing 'Me and My Winstons,' and I began singing it too, and that protected us, for a moment, from the terrible thing that might have happened . . .

And there is brain damage in Arizona, and brain damage in Maine, and little towns in Idaho are in the grip of it, and my blue heaven is black with it, brain damage covering everything like an unbreakable lease –

Skiing along on the soft surface of brain damage, never to sink, because we don't understand the danger –

HOW TO APPEAR IN A GOOD LIGHT
TO A WOMAN IN THE STREET

André Breton

```
.   .   .   .   .   .   .   .   .
.   .   .   .   .   .   .   .   .
.   .   .   .   .   .   .   .   .
.   .   .   .   .   .   .   .   .
.   .   .   .   .   .   .   .   .
```

MY FLANNEL KNICKERS

Leonora Carrington

THOUSANDS OF PEOPLE know my flannel knickers, and though I know this may seem flirtatious, it is not. I am a saint.

The 'Sainthood,' I may say, was actually forced upon me. If anyone would like to avoid becoming holy, they should immediately read this entire story.

I live on an island. This island was bestowed upon me by the government when I left prison. It is not a desert island, it is a traffic island in the middle of a busy boulevard, and motors thunder past on all sides day and night.

So . . .

The flannel knickers are well known. They are hung at midday on a wire from the red, green and yellow automatic lights. I wash them every day, and they have to dry in the sun.

Apart from the flannel knickers, I wear a gentleman's tweed jacket for golfing. It was given to me, and the gym shoes. No socks. Many people recoil from my undistinguished appearance, but if they have been told about me (mainly in the Tourist's Guide), they make a pilgrimage, which is quite easy.

Now I must trace the peculiar events that brought me to this condition. Once I was a great beauty and attended all sorts of cocktail-drinking, prize-giving-and-taking, artistic demonstrations and other casually hazardous gatherings organized for the purpose of people wasting other people's time. I was always in demand and my beautiful face would hang suspended over fashionable garments, smiling continually. An ardent heart, however, beat under the fashionable costumes, and this very ardent heart was like an open tap pouring quantities of hot water over anybody who asked. This wasteful process soon took its toll on my beautiful smiling face. My teeth fell out. The original structure of the face became blurred, and then began to fall away from the bones in small, ever-increasing folds. I sat and watched the process with a mixture of slighted vanity and acute depression. I was, I thought, solidly installed in my lunar plexus, within clouds of sensitive vapour.

If I happened to smile at my face in the mirror, I could objectively observe the fact that I had only three teeth left and these were beginning to decay.

Consequently

I went to the dentist. Not only did he cure the three remaining teeth but he also presented me with a set of false teeth, cunningly mounted on a pink plastic chassis. When I had paid a sufficiently large quantity of my diminishing wealth, the teeth were mine and I took them home and put them into my mouth.

The Face seemed to regain some of its absolutely-irresistible-attraction, although the folds were of course still there. From the lunar plexus I arose like a hungry trout and was caught fast on the sharp barbed hook that hangs inside all once-very-beautiful faces.

A thin magnetic mist formed between myself, the face, and clear perception. This is what I saw in the mist. 'Well, well. I really was beginning to petrify in that old lunar plexus. This must be me, this beautiful, smiling fully toothed creature. There I was, sitting in the dark bloodstream like a mummified foetus with no love at all. Here I am, back in the rich world, where I can palpitate again, jump up and down in the nice warm swimming pool of outflowing emotion, the more bathers the merrier. I Shall Be Enriched.'

All these disastrous thoughts were multiplied and reflected in the magnetic mist. I stepped in, wearing my face, now back in the old enigmatic smile which had always turned sour in the past.

No sooner trapped than done.

Smiling horribly, I returned to the jungle of faces, each ravenously trying to eat each other.

Here I might explain the process that actually takes place in this sort of jungle. Each face is provided with greater or smaller mouths, armed with different kinds of sometimes natural teeth. (Anybody over forty and toothless should be sensible enough to be quietly knitting an original new body, instead of wasting the cosmic wool.) These teeth bar the way to a gaping throat, which disgorges whatever it swallows back into the foetid atmosphere.

The bodies over which these faces are suspended serve as ballast to the faces. As a rule they are carefully covered with colours and shapes in current 'Fashion.' This 'fashion' is a devouring idea launched by another face snapping with insatiable hunger for money and notoriety. The bodies, in constant misery and supplication, are generally ignored and only used for ambulation of the face. As I said, for ballast.

Once, however, that I bared my new teeth I realized that something had gone wrong. For after a very short period of enigmatic smiling, the smile became quite stiff and fixed, while the face slipped away from its bonish mooring, leaving me clutching desperately to a soft grey mask over a barely animated body.

The strange part of the affair now reveals itself. The jungle faces, instead of recoiling in horror from what I already knew to be a sad sight, approached me and started to beg me for something which I thought I had not got.

Puzzled, I consulted my Friend, a Greek.

He said: 'They think you have woven a complete face and body and are in constant possession of excess amounts of cosmic wool. Even if this is not so, the very fact that you know about the wool makes them determined to steal it.'

'I have wasted practically the entire fleece,' I told him. 'And if anybody steals from me now I shall die and disintegrate totally.'

'Three-dimensional life,' said the Greek, 'is formed by

attitude. Since by their attitude they expect you to have quantities of wool, you are three-dimensionally forced to "Sainthood," which means you must spin your body and teach the faces how to spin theirs.'

The compassionate words of the Greek filled me with fear. I am a face myself. The quickest way of retiring from social Face-eating competition occurred to me when I attacked a policeman with my strong steel umbrella. I was quickly put into prison, where I spent months of health-giving meditation and compulsive exercise.

My exemplary conduct in prison moved the Head Wardress to an excess of bounty, and that is how the Government presented me with the island, after a small and distinguished ceremony in a remote corner of the Protestant Cemetery.

So here I am on the island with all sizes of mechanical artifacts whizzing by in every conceivable direction, even overhead.

Here I sit.

'Ah, you must be Surreal McCoy'

UNACCEPTABLE MIXTURE

Leopoldo Chariarse

D URING THE SUMMER of 1947, in one of the rare moments of lucidity permitted me by the routine of lowly bureaucratic employment, I decided to travel through the Amazon forests, to live in nature, among savages, to learn to handle the bow, to eat unknown animals, fruit of incredible shape, the larvae of insects and the roots of trees never seen.

After a brief stay in Yurimaguas where, despite the suffocating heat, I was able to sleep a little, I took my place in the cabin of the hydroplane that had brought me from Masisea and was to take me to my destination, when a traveler occupying the seat to my right – a bald man, with spectacles and something about him of the attorney or the ecclesiastic – asked me:

'Do you know how many planes have come down this year on our route?'

As I had no idea, I declared brutally:

'Ours will make it a half-dozen.'

I told him not to worry, that it was a fair figure, in keeping with the air traffic in that part of the world – one to four per week according to the size of the airline and ours being one of the biggest had more accidents.

My reasoning seemed to offend him. He affirmed that he was not afraid, that he did not need to be calmed down with statistics (for I was explaining that according to the normal curve of accident distribution per unit of time, place, etc.) and that anyway, in spite of completely unfavorable probabilities, it was not death he feared, but desecration of his remains, that at the hands of the savages his flesh might be chopped, ground, salted, or submitted to other treatment incompatible with the dignity of his position.

'*I*, imagine, a representative of judiciary power, a man without vices, without debts!'

I had to assure him that cannibalism was dying out as evangelization made progress and that after all it was more useful to be eaten by other men than devoured by worms, ants, and piranha.

'Don't be too sure,' he exclaimed. 'You know very well that in this part of the forest, evangelization has made no progress since the Indians were obliged to work on plantations.'

I confined myself to a nod, so as to be able to admire in peace the somber greenery of the forest standing out between the blue and grayish mist over the fiery line of the horizon.

I took a room at a little hotel near the river whose waters I could see from my window stretching away out of sight.

It was a quiet inn; scarcely any travelers were in the lounge and on the terrace, and I was already rejoicing at having come at such a favorable season when deafening cries, rising above the sound of the motor of a big bus, made me see my error.

They were getting out in herds, brandishing their movie and snapshot cameras, photographing in all directions, chewing gum, speaking English, noisily opening and closing doors.

They all asked for precise information on the Maracaburus, while the guide discussed the price of rooms with the proprietress.

I knew vaguely that the Indians of that tribe were the mortal enemies of the Carajones, from whom they had learned, however, the art of preparing a large number of magic philters and subtle varieties of curare. Every month, except during the rainy season, they would come down in their canoes, headed for the village markets along the river bank, to sell their well-known salted meats, their medicinal herbs, and also, though secretly, their poisons that earned them the respect of future inconsolable widows in the area.

While I was telling all this, one of the tourists came up and asked me if they sold shrunken heads here and how high the prices could run.

I was going to reply when the hotel owner, who spoke English too, intervened:

'Here, no. You'll find those in Lima, in stores selling antiques and native curios.'

The moment I was preparing to contradict him – for a short distance away, according to what I had been told in Yurimaguas, there was an encampment of Jivaros who kept up a constant trade with the whites, to whom they sold shrunken heads, and with the other Indians from whom they obtained freshly severed ones – he took me by the arm and said to me in an undertone, in Spanish:

'Don't tell them anything. Don't you see that with their mania for carrying off heads they are setting off real massacres among the Indians? For fear of reprisals the latter don't dare refuse to sell any and, as they have none in stock, they are compelled to make them.'

'Aren't they stimulated, rather, by profit? No merchant is obliged to meet demand completely,' I observed.

'You don't know perhaps, but the Indians remember very well what atrocities were committed against them, when they didn't bring in the rate of rubber the English demanded of them. And now when a gang of Americans come insisting upon having the heads of whites, they fall into a panic and go looking for them where they can. They are dubbed savages for having decapitated a few monks and settlers. I don't wish to defend them, but if *my* head was cut off to be sold to tourists I'd know whose fault it was. The Maracaburus, for example, gentle and peaceable by nature, but tributaries of the Jivaros and obliged to supply them with heads, have become cannibals only so as not to let what remains of their prisoners go to waste.'

At that moment a lady interrupted the hotel owner's speech to ask if, further into the interior, it would not be possible for her to obtain a pair of very little heads, children's heads for example, to hang in the rear of her car. White children, she was saying, and French if any could be found. She adored little French children ever since seeing and hearing the 'little singers of the wooden cross.'

The hotel owner raised his eyes to heaven and left me alone

with her. She was a rather fat lady, still young and beautiful. When she spoke there was such enthusiasm in her voice that the sincerity of her love for children could not be doubted.

She told me she belonged to various philanthropic organizations, societies for the protection of animals and waifs and that, in her house in Miami, she had a large collection of tropical fish.

I told her not to worry, that in Lima she would get all the child heads she could wish for, at moderate prices and, who knows, perhaps even French children's heads or Canadian ones from one of the planes come down in the jungle.

I went out that very morning to walk along the river bank. On the right, at the end of an embankment lined with trees, there was a little square in the middle of which, towering above the tops of the coconut palms, rose a sort of column slightly curved. It was an immense cylinder of granite that gave the disorienting feeling of an anachronism or of some monstrous mixture.

Why, indeed, is that phallus – which would not have been out of place in the ruins of Delphi or Mycenae – here, lost in this Christian village on the banks of the Amazon? Was it not an obscure mythological allusion linked with the Amazon seen by Orellana?[1]

Stepping back a little to see from a better angle, I noted that this gigantic member was without its testicles, something that could easily be explained by the prudishness of the authorities. Moreover the glans was missing also, or was hardly indicated perhaps because of a praiseworthy effort at stylization by the artist, tending to anticipate the zeal of an always vigilant censorship.

An inscription similar to that which expresses the public's gratitude to citizens who have fallen at the front only increased my confusion.

It was a monument erected in homage to the martyrs

---

[1] The traveler who first discovered the Amazon and first followed it downstream.

sacrificed by the Maracaburus on the field of honor of Christian faith. There followed a long list of reverend fathers and monks of various orders and numerous military men comprising four lieutenants, fourteen non-commissioned officers, and innumerable soldiers and policemen.

While I was reading the columns set out in strict alphabetical order according to rank, there appeared, dressed all in black, a little old woman making her way sadly but with an indescribably graceful carriage. She approached the railing protecting the monument and dropped a few flowers near the plaque, into a sort of metal box put there for that purpose. Seeing her, I thought I could hear a military band in the distance and a feeling of great tenderness would have come over me if, raising my eyes to the sky, I had not seen that inexorable shape defying all pity.

A most passionate interest followed my initial curiosity upon seeing the old woman's hair combed in a manner that brought to mind irresistibly a Greek hairstyle.

I approached her – a bacchante or a weeping figure exiled at the foot of this last vestige of her divinity – and, to say something, asked her – this is explained by my complete confusion – what day it was and the name of that place.

'Martyrs' Square,' she said smiling and she added, 'Every time I come back here, it seems I am going mad. I couldn't tell you what day it is, Sir. Excuse me.'

Back at the hotel I demanded that the proprietress tell me for what reason, in Martyrs' Square, a pagan sign commemorated the death of these holy men.

She explained that this monument did not represent a male member at all but a sausage.

Faced with my amazement, the good woman confirmed:

'It's because of the victims transformed into sausages by the Maracaburus.

'The best pork-butchers in the area,' added the proprietress' husband who was reading a newspaper, his elbows on the counter.

'Did that event take place a long time ago?' I asked with a certain uneasiness, irritated by the hotel owner's remark.

'Exactly three years,' he replied, giving up reading. 'Since then the hamlet of Maracaburu, a couple of miles from here, is one of the most prosperous places of pilgrimage in the whole country. During the busy season, we don't have enough room to put up all the pilgrims.'

'In spite of the new hotel that's been built,' added the hotel owner's wife bitterly. 'Just imagine, we have to put mats and hammocks out, even in the dining room!'

At lunch, I was introduced to Father Saravia. The hotel proprietor told him I had arrived from Lima and did not know the story of the miracle that the martyrs' remains had occasioned.

'Don Pedro Irribáuregui – a relative of mine – had just been appointed bishop of the region,' said the father, 'when he summoned me to come immediately so that he could ask me to inquire into an event of which the theological and practical implications presented the most unreal and grotesque appearance.

'It had been discovered that a group of Maracaburu Indians had cut up and mixed the flesh of numerous priests, soldiers, and policemen with that of pigs and dogs stolen from the farms in neighboring villages. I had to find out how it was possible to grant those remains Christian burial and, first of all, establish if such a thing had been possible.'

A captain traveling in the direction of the frontier sat down at our table. Of indeterminate age, but fitting his uniform perfectly, he greeted us in friendly fashion, declared that his name was Mirasoles and that he was a member of a commission charged with determining where the frontier ran, through zones about which the treaties in force left some doubt. It was certainly not the least curious aspect of the question to see the two countries in dispute over regions inhabited by cannibal tribes, each claiming the land but affirming that the cannibals were natives of the neighboring country. This contradiction

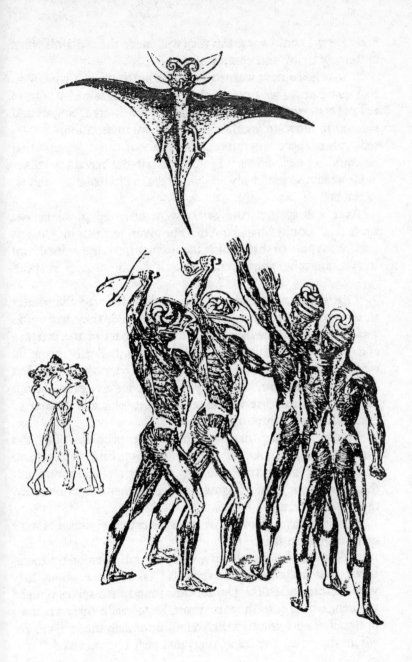

and others I could not grasp very well made the captain's work extremely tiring and complicated.

When the captain learned from the hotel owner's wife, who had come up to wait on us, that Father Saravia had begun to tell me a story, he asked to be excused for interrupting us and wanted to move to another table, but we invited him to stay, telling him there was nothing secret about this story and that he could, in fact, be useful to us in clarifying certain details.

He accepted gratefully and we prepared to listen to the rest of the tale.

'As I was saying,' the priest went on, 'the problem was agonizing. Could Christian burial be given remains in which it was impossible to distinguish the human from the animal, not to mention other ingredients it would be too painful to speak of.'

'That's the easiest thing in the world,' declared the soldier to whom every problem seemed simple. 'All they had to do was determine the exact amount of each part of the mixture and divide each sausage accordingly, symbolically bringing together the parts corresponding to the clergy, the army, and the animal kingdom, and bury them separately, even though in reality the mixture was inextricable. It was all a matter of establishing the proportions exactly.'

'You've said it: that was the whole problem. But the Maracaburus, jealous of their manufacturing secrets and fearing that other tribes might appropriate these and cut them out of the market, would rather let themselves be killed than reveal them.'

'But how was it known that the Maracaburus' sausages were made of human flesh?'

'A few missionaries having disappeared, someone remembered that a comparable event had taken place about fifty years before, when the Dominicans found themselves obliged to change the route they used to take to reach their missions in Brazil. There resulted such a famine among the Indians, for whom they were the staple diet, that very few survived.'

'I know,' interjected the captain. 'Driven by hunger, they crossed the frontier and began attacking villages and plantations. They'd have got as far as Iquitos if they'd not been stopped by the heroic resistance of our troops who, aided by the settlers, in the end exterminated them.'

'To get back to my story, when the disappearances reached alarming proportions, the police scoured the whole region in question but with no other result than the disappearance of numerous policemen.'

'That's when the army stepped in,' exulted Mirasoles, filling out his uniform once again so that it seemed to have more buttons than ever.

'The result was the disappearance of almost a whole regiment,' the priest continued imperturbably.

I thought of that little old women's flowers and those four lieutenants,' fourteen non-commissioned officers, and I don't know how many soldiers mentioned on the plaque that seemed to me terribly human, almost familiar.

But the captain replied:

'All the same, it was thanks to us that the Indians confessed to having killed the missionaries.'

'Finally the dreadful version of the facts had to be admitted and some Indians confessed, spontaneously or out of fear of being interrogated, that they had taken part in the massacre.'

'Immediate seizure of the meat brought in by the savages was then decreed,' thundered Mirasoles again, taking the opportunity to explain his role in detail. 'At that time I was just a lieutenant,' he said modestly.

With dinner behind us, we went to sip coffee on the terrace. The man in spectacles, who knew Mirasoles and Saravia, came up to our table and joined in the conversation. We felt he was very agitated. He told us he had received several threatening letters over a case involving tradespeople, in which he was to act as mediator.

Father Saravia went on:

'As soon as confiscation had been completed in fairs and

markets, interment of the remains was carried out, with no distinction, in a common grave, and the names of the victims were inscribed on a plaque. Mgr. Irribáuregui, who presided over the ceremony, pronounced a moving eulogy. He deplored the absence of the heads and regretted there was no hope of retrieving them, for the Jivaros were uncompromising and it would have been necessary to buy a large quantity from them to separate the heads of civilized people and identify them. This obviously called for special government funds and the cooperation of all the faithful in the province. He would take this matter up: he was counting on the understanding of the government and the generosity of all.

'On the morning of the third day the grave was found to be open and there was complete consternation when it was known that the remains had disappeared. A mixture of terror and indignation ran through clergy and settlers. The military and the police were placed on alert. A curfew was imposed and several Indians shot down in the vicinity.

'The massacre threatened to imperil the whole district's economy if the native population, which does the heavy work and constitutes the main tourist attraction, was decimated,' Mirasoles observed pertinently.

'Divine mercy,' Saravia continued, 'permitted a group of Indians to manage to get to the bishop and relate the event they had all witnessed. Returning to their huts, a little after midnight, they said, a blinding light took them by surprise and while the night was rent by lightning and trumpet music, they had seen the tomb open and the sausages rise up to heaven.

'Mgr. Irribáuregui gave up his return flight to Iquitos that day, and, calling together clergy and people of standing, solemnly announced the miracle.

'Great festivities were organized and, in everyone's joy, the Indians who were to be executed for having participated in the massacres and in salting the meat were allowed to escape. The erection of a monument was decided upon immediately and Mgr. Irribáuregui insisted upon its being given the shape of a sausage.

'Out of respect for his dignity as a prelate and his venerable age we accepted this idea that seemed to us absurd and terribly ridiculous. To our timid objections he replied that it would be a lesson in modesty to the flesh and an example of what man is capable of who has entered the bosom of Christianity.

'Time has borne out what the bishop said, for the number of pilgrims has not stopped rising from year to year and there is already talk of building a basilica.'

His story over, Father Saravia consulted his watch, declared he had to go to work, and left.

Scarcely had he gone when the man with spectacles turned to me and, with a sinister air, said:

'What the good priest doesn't know is that the next day, in all the markets and shops selling food, the famous sausages appeared once again. Housewives were buying them, we were eating them, and no one thought that those who claimed to have witnessed a miracle were the same ones who had sold them. Serious rivalry between tradespeople allowed me to learn the truth. In my capacity as magistrate I did all I could to conceal it, so as to avoid a scandal, but the explosion is inevitable.'

THE ANGRY STREET

G. K. Chesterton

I CANNOT REMEMBER whether this tale is true or not. If I read it through very carefully I have a suspicion that I should come to the conclusion that it is not. But, unfortunately, I cannot read it through very carefully, because, you see, it is not written yet. The image and idea of it clung to me through a great part of my boyhood; I may have dreamt it before I could talk; or told it to myself before I could read; or read it before I could remember. On the whole, however, I am certain that I did not read it. For children have very clear memories about things like that; and of the books of which I was really fond I can still remember not only the shape and bulk and binding, but even the position of the printed words on many of the pages. On the whole, I incline to the opinion that it happened to me before I was born.

At any rate, let us tell the story now with all the advantages of the atmosphere that has clung to it. You may suppose me, for the sake of argument, sitting at lunch in one of those quick-lunch restaurants in the City where men take their food so fast that it has none of the quality of food, and take their half-hour's vacation so fast that it has none of the qualities of leisure. To hurry through one's leisure is the most unbusiness-like of actions. They all wore tall shiny hats as if they could not lose an instant even to hang them on a peg, and they all had one eye a little off, hypnotized by the huge eye of the clock. In short they were the slaves of the modern bondage, you could hear their fetters clanking. Each was, in fact, bound by a chain; the heaviest chain ever tied to a man – it is called a watch-chain.

Now, among these there entered and sat down opposite to

me a man who almost immediately opened an uninterrupted monologue. He was like all the other men in dress, yet he was startlingly opposite to them all in manner. He wore a high shiny hat and a long frock coat, but he wore them as such solemn things were meant to be worn; he wore the silk hat as if it were a mitre, and the frock coat as if it were the ephod of a high priest. He not only hung his hat up on the peg, but he seemed (such was his stateliness) almost to ask permission of the hat for doing so, and to apologize to the peg for making use of it. When he had sat down on a wooden chair with the air of one considering its feelings and given a sort of slight stoop or bow to the wooden table itself, as if it were an altar, I could not help some comment springing to my lips. For the man was a big, sanguine-faced, prosperous-looking man, and yet he treated everything with a care that almost amounted to nervousness.

For the sake of saying something to express my interest I said, 'This furniture is fairly solid; but, of course, people do treat it much too carelessly.'

As I looked up doubtfully my eye caught his, and was fixed as his was fixed, in an apocalyptic stare. I had thought him ordinary as he entered, save for his strange, cautious manner; but if the other people had seen him then they would have screamed and emptied the room. They did not see him, and they went on making a clatter with their forks, and a murmur with their conversation. But the man's face was the face of a maniac.

'Did you mean anything particular by that remark?' he asked at last, and the blood crawled back slowly into his face.

'Nothing whatever,' I answered. 'One does not mean anything here; it spoils people's digestions.'

He leaned back and wiped his broad forehead with a high handkerchief; and yet there seemed to be a sort of regret in his relief.

'I thought perhaps,' he said in a low voice, 'that another of them had gone wrong.'

59

'If you mean another digestion gone wrong,' I said, 'I never heard of one here that went right. This is the heart of the Empire, and the other organs are in an equally bad way.'

'No, I mean another street gone wrong,' he said heavily and quietly, 'but as I suppose that doesn't explain much to you, I think I shall have to tell you the story. I do so with all the less responsibility; because I know you won't believe it. For forty years of my life I invariably left my office, which is in Leadenhall Street, at half-past five in the afternoon, taking with me an umbrella in the right hand and a bag in the left hand. For forty years two months and four days I passed out of the side office door, walked down the street on the left-hand side, took the first turning to the left and the third to the right, from where I bought an evening paper, followed the road on the right-hand side round two obtuse angles, and came out just outside a Metropolitan station, where I took a train home. For forty years two months and four days I fulfilled this course by accumulated habit: it was not a long street that I traversed, and it took me about four and a half minutes to do it. After forty years two months and four days, on the fifth day I went out in the same manner, with my umbrella in the right hand and my bag in the left, and I began to notice that walking along the familiar street tired me somewhat more than usual. At first I thought I must be breathless and out of condition; though this, again, seemed unnatural, as my habits had always been like clockwork. But after a little while I became convinced that the road was distinctly on a more steep incline that I had known previously; I was positively panting uphill. Owing to this no doubt the corner of the street seemed further off than usual; and when I turned it I was convinced that I had turned down the wrong one. For now the street shot up quite a steep slant, such as one only sees in the hilly parts of London, and in this part there were no hills at all. Yet it was not the wrong street. The name written on it was the same; the shuttered shops were the same; the lamp-posts and the whole look of the perspective was the same; only it was tilted upwards like a lid. Forgetting any trouble about breathlessness or fatigue I ran furiously forward, and reached the second of my accustomed turnings, which ought to bring me almost within sight of the station. And as I turned that corner I nearly fell on the pavement. For now the street went up straight in front of my face like a steep staircase or the side of a pyramid. There was not for miles round that place so much as a slope like that of Ludgate Hill. And this was a slope like that of the Matterhorn. The whole street had lifted itself like a single wave, and yet every speck and detail of it was the same, and I saw in the high distance, as at the top of an Alpine pass, picked out in pink letters the name over my paper shop.

'I ran on and on blindly now, passing all the shops, and coming to a part of the road where there was a long grey row of private houses. I had, I know not why, an irrational feeling that I was on a long iron bridge in empty space. An impulse seized me, and I pulled up the iron trap of a coal hole. Looking down through it I saw empty space and the stars.

'When I looked up again a man was standing in his front garden, having apparently come out of his house; he was leaning over the railings and gazing at me. We were all alone on that nightmare road; his face was in shadow; his dress was dark and ordinary; but when I saw him standing so perfectly still I knew somehow that he was not of this world. And the stars behind his head were larger and fiercer than ought to be endured by the eyes of men.

' "If you are a kind angel," I said, "or a wise devil, or have anything in common with mankind, tell me what is this street possessed of devils."

'After a long silence he said, "What do you say that it is?"

' "It is Bumpton Street, of course," I snapped. "It goes to Oldgate Station."

' "Yes," he admitted gravely; "it goes there sometimes. Just now, however, it is going to heaven."

' "To heaven?" I said. "Why?"

' "It is going to heaven for justice," he replied. "You must

have treated it badly. Remember always that there is one thing that cannot be endured by anybody or anything. That one unendurable thing is to be overworked and also neglected. For instance, you can overwork women – everybody does. But you can't neglect women – I defy you to. At the same time, you can neglect tramps and gipsies and all the apparent refuse of the State, so long as you do not overwork them. But no beast of the field, no horse, no dog can endure long to be asked to do more than his work and yet have less than his honour. It is the same with streets. You have worked this street to death, and yet you have never remembered its existence. If you had owned a healthy democracy, even of pagans, they would have hung this street with garlands and given it the name of a god. Then it would have gone quietly. But at last the street has grown tired of your tireless insolence; and it is bucking and rearing its head to heaven. Have you never sat on a bucking horse?"

'I looked at the long grey street, and for a moment it seemed to me to be exactly like the long grey neck of a horse flung up to heaven. But in a moment my sanity returned, and I said, "But this is all nonsense. Streets go to the place they have to go to. A street must always go to its end."

' "Why do you think so of a street?' he asked, standing very still.

' "Because I have always seen it do the same thing," I replied, in reasonable anger. "Day after day, year after year, it has always gone to Oldgate Station; day after . . ."

'I stopped, for he had flung up his head with the fury of the road in revolt.

' "And you?" he cried terribly. "What do you think the road thinks of you? Does the road think you are alive? Are you alive! Day after day, year after year, *you* have gone to Oldgate Station . . ." Since then I have respected the things called inanimate.'

And bowing slightly to the mustard-pot, the man in the restaurant withdrew.

THE MANIKIN WITH THE SUGAR NOSE

Salvador Dali

A ND NOW CLICK your tongues with satisfaction against your palates, producing that sound of the uncorking of a bottle, so agreeable to the ears, for I myself am about to uncork the full bottles that you all are, and I intend this evening to get completely drunk on the avid alcohol of your curiosity.

I am about to begin . . . I begin . . . We have begun!

Once upon a time there was a king whose manner of life was very strange. Each day there were brought to him three of the most beautiful girls in the kingdom who had to come and water the sweet-williams in his garden. From the top of his tower he would look down upon them, and hesitate long before choosing her who should spend the night in the royal bed, around which perfumed oils burned. She would be adorned with the most precious robes and jewels, and would have to sleep, or feign to sleep, through the whole night. The king never touched her, only looked at her. But when dawn rose, he would cut off her head with a single blow of his sabre.

To designate his choice, the king would address her whom he singled out to be the victim of his night of 'unfulfilled love,' and leaning over the rampart of the tower he invariably asked her this same question,

'How many sweet-williams are there in my garden?'

And the girl, who by this question learned her death sentence, had to lower her eyes in shame, and invariably answer him with malice this other question,

'How many stars are there in the sky?'

After which the king would disappear. The chosen girl would run to her house, where her weeping parents adorned her with her richest garments in preparation for her macabre nuptial night.

One day the king's choice fell on a girl whose beauty and intelligence were renowned throughout the kingdom. Now this girl, whose intelligence was as resplendent as her beauty, when she learned that she had been chosen, made a wax manikin to which she glued a sugar nose.

When night arrived she draped herself in a white sheet, and, hiding the manikin within it, went up into the nuptial chamber in which all the candles were lit. She placed the wax manikin with the sugar nose on the bed, covering it with her most beautiful jewels. After which she lay down under the bed, and waited.

When the king entered he stripped himself naked, and lay down beside her whom he thought he had chosen. He spent the whole night in looking at her, but as usual he did not touch her. Also, as usual, the moment he sensed the coming dawn he unsheathed his sword and with a single blow cut off the head of the wax manikin. With the blow the sugar nose broke off and flew right into the king's mouth. Surprised by the sweetness of the sugar nose the king dolefully cried,

> *Dulcetta en vida,*
> *Dulcetta en mor,*
> *Si t'agues coneguda*
> *No t'auria mort!*

Which means literally,

> *Sweet in life,*
> *Sweet in death,*
> *If I had known you*
> *I should not have given you death!*

At this moment the wily beauty, who had heard everything from beneath the bed, quickly came forth, presenting herself to the king and unveiling her stratagem to him.

The king, suddenly and miraculously cured of his criminal aberration, married her, and they lived happily for many long years.

And there the tale ends.

INTERPRETATION OF THE TALE OF THE WAX MANIKIN WITH THE SUGAR NOSE

Let us try now to interpret this story in the light that psychoanalysis by my own original methods of investigation can shed upon it.

We shall begin with the generating element of the stratagem, the wax manikin with the sugar nose, and first of all, with the wax itself as a clearly characteristic and determining element.

I shall first recall to your mind its livid color, as evidenced in the expression 'wan, or pale, as wax,' and the current assimilation of this pallor to that of death; also its ductile consistency (a kind of imitation flesh). Wax is furthermore not only the matter that lends itself best to the imitation of living forms and figures, but also that which succeeds in imitating them in the most anguishing fashion – that is to say, the one which, while being the most life-like, is at the same time the most inert, the most spectral, and in short the most macabre (witness the artificial cemeteries which the morbid museums of wax figures constitute, especially the Musée Grevin in Paris). The non-repugnant character of wax, which is further augmented by an attractive softness, has a variety of reasons far more direct and less intellectual than that of its con-substantiality with the honey from which it originally derives. This softness of wax, moreover, is partially due to its extreme ductility, reaching the state of liquefaction upon exposure to heat – which is not a property of so many other malleable substances (clay, etc.) which on the contrary have a tendency to dry and harden. This liquefaction, with the defiguration which it entails, may easily appear as characteristic of the decomposition of corpses.

We shall furthermore observe that even when wax most obviously evokes decomposition, as would be the case of a wax manikin if it should melt, this would nevertheless always occur without provoking repugnance, in place of which one would be conscious of a gentle anguish, owing to the fact that this would constitute the most pleasant and attenuated fashion of representing such a state. It is as if on every occasion and under all circumstances the evocation of death transmitted by the mediation and vehicle of wax were able to affect us in the gentlest fashion and constituted a pseudo-sweet used to make us 'swallow' a great terror. Throughout all anecdotology of the macabre and funereal rites wax does not cease for a moment to play this constant, deceptive and attenuating role to which we have just called attention, shedding light upon the dead with a false and attractive light of desirable life beneath the quivering flames of the candles that are being consumed.

Still upon this vertiginous slope of my hypothesis, it is necessary to imagine the necrophile madly troubled by the odor of burning wax which, replacing that of the sweat of the loved being lying inert, without sweat, without odor of life, would serve to render more desirable the blended, incipient and real odor of death, by attenuating it and providing it with that substitute and euphemistic illusion necessary to the nostalgic pleasure of the necrophilic 'passional aberration.'

The wax, then, by its softening and idealized representation of death, would serve to prepare the short-cut to necrophilic impulses and desires. Furthermore it would act as a sentinel to the mechanism of repression, keeping out of the sphere of consciousness the coprophagic phantasms which in a more or less veiled fashion commonly coexist with the 'desire for waste matter.' Thus the hypocritical warmth of the wax in a symbolic situation would replace the atrocious crudity of the

67

real intention of these phantasms, with all the candles of copro-necrophilic consummation already lighted for the nuptial feast which would couple these two passions that together constitute the peak of aberration and perversity.[1]

Returning to our tale, we must observe that the extremely flagrant necrophilic sentiments of the king led him to anticipate his final and decisive act by a whole appropriate ritual destined to envelop the 'expectant and unfulfilled' love which was to precede the fatal *dénouement*. It was necessary – as we learned – for the king's victim to spend the night in a state of immobility; she had to sleep or feign to sleep – in short, she had to play dead. The king's fantasy further commanded that the sleeping girl remain prone *on* the sheets, adorned with rare and dazzling robes, like a corpse. Also it is specified that perfumed oils would be burning in the nuptial chamber and that 'all the candles' must be lighted (as for the dead). All this neurotic preamble obviously had no other aim than to furnish, by a series of mortuary simulacra, idealized representations of his pathological case, in order that the victim be imagined as having already expired, well before the culminating moment in which, as in a definitive and material 'realization of desire the king reached the point of really killing the desired dead woman with his weapon, and this in the finally consummated paroxysm of his pleasure – which, in his aberration, coincided with the very moment of ejaculation.

But just at this supreme moment the tale tells us that the wily beauty who had substituted the wax manikin for herself behaved intuitively like a refined and extremely skilful expert in the most modern psychological sciences. What she did was to effect the miraculous cure of her husband-to-be by a substitutive operation which could be regarded only as magical. The wax manikin must have appeared to the king

---

[1] A very precise study of the wax candle, written in 1929, led me to the conclusion that this object lends itself to a whole series of symbolic situations in which non-terrorizing unconscious representations of intestinal and digestive metaphors lead to the apotheosis of human waste matter – the turd.

as the deadest of all his beautiful girls, and at the same time the most special, the most life-like, the most softened, desired and 'metaphysical' of all. The nose falling off, a defiguration genuinely evocative of death, must also by its possible links with and recalls of the castration complex have reactualized his fears of punishment, while at the same time preparing an ambiance of remorse which by the tension of guilt feelings was propitious to an imminent repentance. The king, probably a cannibalistic copro-necrophile, was at bottom only seeking to savor the true hidden taste of death, his censor allowing him to achieve this only through the appearance of a false life composed of the pseudo-sleep of the wax with its macabre ornamentation and display. The sugared taste of the nose, falling unexpectedly into his mouth, can only have been a startling anticlimax, something incongruously inadequate and paradoxical, causing him to react in the same way as, in the inverse case, the nursing child reacts when he is being weaned.[1] The child finds his mother's nipple suddenly offering a bitter, disagreeable and nauseating taste instead of the agreeable one of the milk he was expecting. He does not want to repeat this experience; after the cruel disappointment he no longer wants to suck his mother's breast.

The king wanted to eat corpse, and instead of the taste of corpse he found that of sugar, after which he no longer wanted to eat corpse. But in addition to this the 'sugar nose' of our tale played a much more subtle and decisive role than that of having succeeded in weaning our king from death. It did not indeed correspond to the secretly desired taste of death, but this disappointment was only partially and relatively disagreeable. For it did not only become a lucid element of cannibalistic consciousness. Most important of all, the fact that this disappointment was experienced at the very moment of pleasure (as is the case in hysterical fits) operated

---

[1] The author is here referring to the formerly very wide-spread method of weaning children by coating the nursing mother's nipples with a substance of disagreeable taste. [Translator's note]

in such a way as to re-evaluate instantaneously and with the maximum of violence the reality of a sweetness unexpected and unknown, 'effective' and 'sensible' in reality – in life a sweetness which could suddenly appear and become desirable, precisely because the sugar nose had just served as a 'bridge' to desire, enabling it to pass from death to life. Thus the king's whole libidinous discharge formed an unfaithful fixation upon life, since this real sweetness was that which by surprise happened to occupy the expected place which the fictive sweetness of death was to occupy.

> Sweet in life,
> Sweet in death,
> If I had known you
> I should not have given you death . . .

A wholly spontaneous way (since involuntarily the word 'life' occurs in the first line, in spite of being but a consequence of and a deduction from the second line) of expressing the regret at 'having killed her,' which confirms the prevision of the cure of the king's psychic disturbances.

MEET MY MAKER

J. P. Donleavy

I SET OUT one summer singing. To meet my Maker. He lived on a hill with lawns around and buttercups sprinkled in the green. I said I'll climb your hill and knock on your door, look in your windows and see what I saw. He came out in a pair of blue jeans with a pipe and said hi, when did you die.

I told him yesterday about noon. They all stood around for my doom. Even Sidney in his sun glasses and Flora just out of her red sports car. They looked at me and said he's gone for a ride and that's all I heard when I died.

And Maker said come in and sit down. He said sherry. I said pale please and dry. Now tell me young man how was your trip, were some of the stops called despair and did you see the town called sad. Or did you detour through laugh. Maker I'll tell you the truth I stayed too long in the metropolis called money which I found to be sunny, a city of aspic, tinkle and titters where I bought at the bottom and sold at the top.

But son surely you didn't stay. Maker I did and never left till my dying day. I lived way up in the sky with a terrace where I sang my song:

> Every tulip
> Is a julep
> And all the mint
> Is meant for me.

And Sidney and Flora came and said why don't we have some fun and go up to Vermont for a barbecue. And all night we drove through the beer cans along the road. I sat looking out between the trees and at others racing along and I thought I'm weak and want to belong. To clubs and leisure life and breathe only imported air. But Flora said I was the sensitive type who looked well with a pipe and could afford to be poor if I wanted or even maybe something real special so that they'd all be glad to know me later on. But I said no I want to be loved for my money and nothing else will do. So off we went to Vermont for the barbecue.

Out by the lake we lit a fire, spread out the marshmallow and steak. And Maker this is why I never had a chance to repent. I just thought I'd go for a swim and look up at the stars and then sat around and got a chill and later I knew I was ill. So I said before I was dead take me back to the city of money fast and see how much they charge to get out of this. And they came and said buddy you're on your way to the next town and this here train can't turn round. So I said where's the ticket taker maybe he personally knows my Maker because I have a few things he can buy at the bottom. But they said there is no ticket taker because this ride's free.

So Maker I just said gee and as you can see I never had courage to give up the salmon and riesling or the picnics at Newport but stayed at my club for showers and grub and could never get enough. Son, cheer up, I know how you feel, but let me tell you we have some fine vintages here as well as delectable veal. And oceans of time and beef in its prime. So relax and watch the sun shine. But Maker how can you welcome me from that land down there when I've never been kind or felt any despair. Son, I can see you never meant any harm, another helping of the peaches and cream is no need for alarm.

But Maker, what about Sidney and Flora. Son, come over, you can see them from here. Wow, Maker, can you see all this. Son, behind every and any blind. But Sidney's got my cigarette lighter and Flora my flat, why those cheapskates, I'll never forgive them for that. Easy son, that's what you were like before you got up here. But Sidney's playing my gramophone and Flora's taken my Ming horse. Son, next time leave nothing behind and you'll feel no remorse.

Well, Maker, what do we do now. Son, it's time for a swim and workout in the gym and after a good scrub I'll take you to a nightclub. But Maker I can't see how we so readily agree, this is even better than it was down there and it's free. Son, look me in the eye and see what you see. Whoa, Maker, you're me.

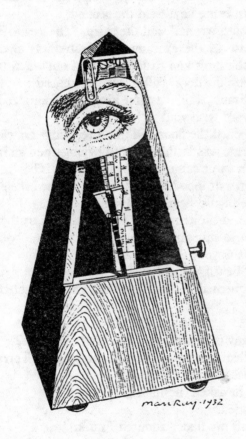

THE KEY IS FRANK

Bob Dylan

THERE WERE THREE kings and a jolly three too. The first one had a broken nose, the second a broken arm and the third was broke. 'Faith is the key!' said the first king.

'No, froth is the key!' said the second.

'You're both wrong,' said the third. 'The key is Frank!'

It was late in the evening and Frank was sweeping up, preparing the meat and dishing himself out when there came a knock upon the door. 'Who is it?' he mused.

'It's us, Frank,' said the three kings in unison, 'and we'd like to have a word with you!'

Frank opened the door and the three kings crawled in.

Terry Shute was in the midst of prying open an hairdresser when Frank's wife came in and caught him. 'They're here!' she gasped. Terry dropped his drawer and rubbed the eye.

'What do they appear to be like?'

'One's got a broken vessel, and that's the truth, the other two I'm not so sure about.'

'Fine, thank you, that'll be all.'

'Good.' She turned and puffed.

Terry tightened his belt and in an afterthought stated: 'Wait!'

'Yes?'

'How many of them would you say there were?'

Vera smiled, she tapped her toe three times. Terry watched her foot closely.

'Three?' he asked, hesitating.

Vera nodded.

'Get up off my floor!' shouted Frank.

The second king, who was first to rise, mumbled, 'Where's the better half, Frank?'

Frank, who was in no mood for jokes, took it lightly, replying: 'She's in the back of the house, flaming it up with an arrogant man. Now come on, out with it, what's on our little minds today?'

Nobody answered.

Terry Shute then entered the room with a bang, looking the three kings over and fondling his mop. Getting down to the source of things, he proudly boasted: 'There is a creeping consumption in the land. It begins with these three fellas and it travels outward. Never in my life have I seen such a motley crew. They ask nothing and they receive nothing. Forgiveness is not in them. The wilderness is rotten all over their foreheads. They scorn the widow and abuse the child but I am afraid that they shall not prevail over the young man's destiny, not even them!'

Frank turned with a blast, 'Get out of here, you ragged man! Come ye no more!'

Terry left the room willingly.

'What seems to be the problem?' Frank turned back to the three kings, who were astonished. The first king cleared his throat. His shoes were too big and his crown was wet and lopsided but, nevertheless, he began to speak in the most meaningful way.

'Frank,' he began, 'Mr Dylan has come out with a new record.[1] This record of course features none but his own songs and we understand that you're the key.'

'That's right,' said Frank, 'I am.'

'Well then,' said the king in a bit of excitement, 'Could you please open it up for us?'

Frank, who all this time had been reclining with his eyes closed, suddenly opened them both up as wide as a tiger. 'And just how far would you like to go in?' he asked, and the three kings all looked at each other.

---

[1] *John Wesley Harding*, CBS Records 1968.

'Not too far but just far enough so's we can say that we've been there,' said the first chief.

'All right,' said Frank, 'I'll see what I can do,' and he commenced to doing it.

First of all, he sat down and crossed his legs, then he sprang up, ripped off his shirt and began waving it in the air. A lightbulb fell from one of his pockets, and he stamped it out with his foot. Then he took a deep breath, moaned and punched his fist through the plate glass window. Settling back in his chair, he pulled out a knife. 'Far enough?' he asked.

'Yeah, sure, Frank,' said the second king.

The third king just shook his head and said he didn't know.

The first king remained silent.

The door opened and Vera stepped in. 'Terry Shute will be leaving us soon and he desires to know if you kings got any gifts you wanna lay on him?'

Nobody answered.

It was just before the break of day and the three kings were tumbling along the road. The first one's nose had been mysteriously fixed, the second one's arm had healed and the third one was rich. All three of them were blowing horns. 'I've never been so happy in all my life!' sang the one with all the money.

'Oh mighty thing!' said Vera to Frank. 'Why didn't you just tell them you were a moderate man and leave it at that instead of goosing yourself all over the room?'

'Patience, Vera,' said Frank.

Terry Shute, who was sitting over by the curtain cleaning an axe, climbed to his feet, walked over to Vera's husband and placed his hand on his shoulder.

'Yuh didn't hurt yer hand, didja Frank?'

Frank just sat there watching the workmen replace the window.

'I don't believe so,' he said.

THE PASSION CONSIDERED AS AN UPHILL BICYCLE RACE

Alfred Jarry

BARABBAS, slated to race, was scratched.

Pilate, the starter, pulling out his clepsydra or water clock, an operation which wet his hands unless he had merely spat on them – Pilate gave the send-off.

Jesus got away to a good start.

In those days, according to the excellent sports commentator St. Matthew, it was customary to flagellate the sprinters at the start the way a coachman whips his horses. The whip both stimulates and gives a hygienic massage. Jesus, then, got off in good form; but he had a flat right away. A bed of thorns punctured the whole circumference of his front tire.

Today in the shop windows of bicycle dealers you can see a reproduction of this veritable crown of thorns as an ad for puncture-proof tires. But Jesus's was an ordinary single-tube racing tire.

The two thieves, obviously in cahoots and therefore 'thick as thieves,' took the lead.

It is not true that there were any nails. The three objects usually shown in the ads belong to a rapid-change tire tool called the 'Jiffy.'

We had better begin by telling about the spills; but before that the machine itself must be described.

The bicycle frame in use today is of relatively recent invention. It appeared around 1890. Previous to that time the body of the machine was constructed of two tubes soldered together at right angles. It was generally called the right-angle or cross bicycle. Jesus, after his puncture, climbed the slope on foot, carrying on his shoulder the bike frame, or, if you will, the cross.

Contemporary engravings reproduce this scene from photographs. But it appears that the sport of cycling, as a result of the well known accident which put a grievous end to the Passion race and which was brought up to date almost on its anniversary by the similar accident of Count Zborowski on the Turbie slope – the sport of cycling was for a time prohibited by state ordinance. That explains why the illustrated magazines, in reproducing this celebrated scene, show bicycles of a rather imaginary design. They confuse the machine's cross frame with that other cross, the straight handlebar. They represent Jesus with his hands spread on the handlebars, and it is worth mentioning in this connection that Jesus rode lying flat on his back in order to reduce his air resistance.

Note also that the frame or cross was made of wood, just as wheels are to this day.

A few people have insinuated falsely that Jesus's machine was a *drasienne*,* an unlikely mount for a hill-climbing contest. According to the old cyclophile hagiographers, St. Bridget, St. Gregory of Tours, and St. Irene, the cross was equipped with a device which they name *suppedaneum*. There is no need to be a great scholar to translate this as 'pedal.'

Lipsius, Justinian, Bosius, and Erycius Puteanus describe another accessory which one still finds, according to Cornelius Curtius in 1643, on Japanese crosses: a protuberance of leather or wood on the shaft which the rider sits astride – manifestly the seat or saddle.

This general description, furthermore, suits the definition of a bicycle current among the Chinese: 'A little mule which is led by the ears and urged along by showering it with kicks.'

We shall abridge the story of the race itself, for it has been

---

[1]A two-wheeled, bicycle-like machine without pedals fashionable in 1818. The rider straddled it and paced along with part of his weight on the seat. [Translator's note.]

narrated in detail by specialized works and illustrated by sculpture and painting visible in monuments built to house such art.

There are fourteen turns in the difficult Golgotha course. Jesus took his first spill at the third turn. His mother, who was in the stands, became alarmed.

His excellent trainer, Simon the Cyrenian, who but for the thorn accident would have been riding out in front to cut the wind, carried the machine.

Jesus, though carrying nothing, perspired heavily. It is not certain whether a female spectator wiped his brow, but we know that Veronica, a girl reporter, got a good shot of him with her Kodak.

The second spill came at the seventh turn on some slippery pavement. Jesus went down for the third time at the eleventh turn, skidding on a rail.

The Israelite *demi-mondaines* waved their handkerchiefs at the eighth.

The deplorable accident familiar to us all took place at the twelfth turn. Jesus was in a dead heat at the time with the thieves. We know that he continued the race airborne – but that is another story.

FORTY VISITS TO THE WORM FARM

Frank Key

PART ONE: VISITS ONE TO FIVE

ONE

B Y BICYCLE. A number of the spokes went awry and I had to walk the last half mile. A member of staff at the Worm Farm promised to have the bicycle fixed for me. I handed over a soiled five pound note to cover the cost of repair, and caught the bus home.

TWO

By bus. Thrilled to distraction at the prospect of the return of my trusty bicycle. The past week had been harrowing. I had hardly stepped outside my allotment shed. It was pouring with rain. A party of dishevelled geese had set up a temporary shelter at the entrance to the Worm Farm. The Farm itself was in disarray. Canute Hellhound, Director of Research, had locked himself inside the staff canteen, brandishing a pitchfork and threatening to impale several members of staff on it. Desperate attempts were being made to contact his doctor. I felt ravaged by my insignificance, and left the scene at once. On the bus home, I realised that I did not know the name of the woman who had promised to mend my bicycle, and had only a dim recollection of her appearance.

THREE

The next day. The man who grows turnips on the allotment next to mine offered to give me a lift to the Worm Farm. He said he would be passing that way. In the car, he told me that his son worked as an engineer in Swanage and that his daughter had been awarded the Order of Lenin. I wanted to ask him why he grew nothing but turnips on his plot, but was unable to steer the conversation in the right direction. He was unable to steer his car in the right direction; we arrived at Hooting Yard without having passed the Worm Farm. He seemed dreadfully embarrassed, and began to unfold an enormous road map. It was so dog-eared that the folds threatened to become rips, and in some cases had already done so. His forefinger trailed aimlessly over the map, unable to locate the Worm Farm. He apologised with a sincerity that rattled me. I said that it really didn't matter and that I would find my way on foot. I got out of the car. I had no idea where I was. I spoke to a few passers-by, to ask directions, and was awestruck by their rum accents and bearing. No one was able to help me. I was unnerved by the lopsided gait which seemed to afflict all the inhabitants of Hooting Yard, and by their sickly pallors. I felt as if I was in a foreign land. The smell of turpentine hung heavy in the air. I took refuge in a pub. Instead of carpeting, or floorboards, there was sticky gravel underfoot. The beer tasted vile, but I settled to it, and got riotously drunk – so much so that my memory is impaired. Oh, I get the occasional shudder of recollection – a pack of wolfhounds, two men carrying a winding-sheet, a bottle of bleach with a loose lid – but I am still unable to work out quite what happened. Later that day, or perhaps another day, I don't know, I came to with a massive hangover at my mother's house. She strewed my room with temperance tracts and refused to speak to me for a week.

FOUR

Another abortive trip to the Worm Farm. The bus was waylaid by highwaymen in period costume. They took my watch and an old biro which I treasured. Following this incident, the bus-driver immediately turned around and drove back to the depot to file a full report.

FIVE

Weighed down by a huge roll of baize which I had promised to deliver to my aunt, I waited an hour for the bus. Luckily, the trip passed without incident. Arriving at the Worm Farm, I was met at the gates by Canute Hellhound. He took me to one side and began to declaim at length on the need for more whisks. Something in his manner transfixed me. His high-pitched jabbering, rising to shrieks and howls at particularly pertinent moments in his discourse, was absolutely hypnotic. I think we must have walked around the perimeter fence twelve or thirteen times, as his enthused proclamations made me more and more convinced that there were not enough whisks. Then I realised that I had left my baize on the bus! I panicked and, stammering apologetic rubbish to Hellhound, made off at once to catch the bus to the depot. An hour or so later, I arrived to find that the depot had been struck by lightning. Damage was limited, but my baize had been entirely incinerated. I wept. First my bicycle, which as time went on seemed lost for ever. And now the baize. Perhaps everything I owned that began with B would be taken from me. Some malign figure, hooded no doubt, enwrapped in a grisly shift, would steal away my books, my balaclava, my beekeeping utensils and my blunderbuss. Tears streamed down my face. Perhaps even my breakfast would be whipped away from the table before I had a chance to tuck into it. Ghastly visions of the future swept before me. I swooned.

PART TWO: VISITS SIX TO TEN

SIX

Monday. Canute Hellhound arrived for his first day at work.

Canute Hellhound

He had been overjoyed to gain this appointment: Director of Research at the finest Worm Farm in the land! He drooled at the very thought. He, Canute Impetigo Hellhound, son of humble tourniquet-looseners, had scaled the heights. A sallow urchin ushered him into his office, and the first blow of disappointment hit him. There was too much wood in the room. Nearly all of the furniture and most of the fixtures – all wooden. It could not be countenanced. He must make a firm stand from the very beginning. Beckoning the urchin back into the office, he delivered his first command in ringing tones. 'Fetch me a flame-thrower, you young scalliwag!' roared Hellhound.

SEVEN

Tuesday. Canute Hellhound sat on the floor in the charred shell of his office, dallying with an earwig which he had interrupted in its innocent trek across the room. He wondered if it was a deformed worm. Here was something he could research thoroughly. Placing the earwig in a small dish, he strode off to the lab. It was deserted. Most of the exciting scientific equipment had been packed away higgledy-piggledy in cupboards to make room for about thirty broken bicycles which were strewn all over the lab. Canute Hellhound pondered the meaning of these funny metallic constructions. Heaving one from the floor, he laid it on its side on a worktop and mucked about with the wheels and the saddle-height adjuster. He was deeply impressed. Carefully placing the earwig on one of the flat tyres, he rummaged around in the cupboards until he found the time-lapse photography equipment. It took him all afternoon to set it up. Ah, but what an afternoon! Worth at least a page or two when the definitive history of scientific achievement came to be written. Hellhound beamed smugly. He could feel his destiny beginning to enfold him in its warm and musky wraps.

EIGHT

Wednesday. Hellhound failed to turn up for work. Research at the Worm Farm came to a standstill. At 10.30 a.m. the Personnel and Plumbing Director rang his home. There was no reply. In fact, Canute Hellhound was on the premises. Since the small hours, he had been perched unsteadily on the roof of the Worm Farm Staff Dancehall, whittling away at a plank of wood. From time to time he peered off into the distance through his homemade rubbery telescope. His vantage point afforded him a stupendous view, although a chill had begun to set into his bones.

NINE

Thursday. The pitchfork/canteen incident. Many questions remain. Where did Hellhound acquire the pitchfork? Why did he paint it blue? Whose paint did he use? Was the paint bought or stolen? Was the paint still wet? If so, did it stain Hellhound's hands? Or was he wearing gloves? Of what fabric were the gloves woven? Was it wool? If so, had Hellhound personally sheared a sheep? Did he know how to, without injuring the sheep? If he did injure the sheep, did the sheep survive? If not, was its death mourned? Where was it buried? Did Hellhound accept responsibility? Did he attend a short service in commemoration of the sheep? Did he read out a moving prayer from the pulpit? Was he a religious man at the best of times? When were the best of times? Did Hellhound realise they were the best? Or did he think them merely mediocre? How did he arrive at this judgement? Why was he so averse to wood?

TEN

Friday. Extract from Canute Hellhound's four-hour lecture, delivered to the two thousand staff of the Worm Farm in the Great Assembly Hall. 'Good morning. I stand before you wearing a tweed suit. Tweed suits me, I know. I know too that it is the cloth of weakness, of dispersal, desuetude, and ruin. But I am not here to discuss the language of fabric. I am here to give you the benefit of my long years of research into our friends, the worms. [Flourishes set of superbly intricate diagrams from beneath jacket and hangs them up with clothes-pegs. Talks at length on each diagram. Voice rises with excitement. Eyes become glazed with fanaticism. Arms gesticulate in enthused manner. Says things like:] The glands of the investing tissue secrete lime and deposit it always submerged. These arrest the spat at the moment of emission. They detach with a hook the piles covered with fascines and branches, if we can use the term, buried in the sands or mud, their polypiferous portion sallying into the water. The raches, roughened and furrowed down the middle with pointed spiculae, or tubercular ramifications prolonged in a straight canal, the columellar edge sometimes callous – this is the critical moment for the hapless bivalve! He seizes it with a three-pronged fork, aiding also the functions of the stomach, filled with villainous green matter, which is conical, swollen in the middle, diminished, and tapers off, producing new beings, covered with vibratile cilia, furnished with two fins, limited only by the length of the stem, but in a moment beginning to dissolve its corporation, a soft reticulated crust, or bark, full of little cavities. The hinder ones loosen their hold, with four or six rows of ambulacral pieces designated by the names of compass, plumula, bristling envelope, levelled bayonets, smothered. Last come the terrible and multiplied engines of calcareous immovable thread-like cirrhi with transverse bands, many of which crumble. Sometimes they are dredged. Thank you so much.'

PART THREE: VISITS ELEVEN TO FIFTEEN

ELEVEN

She returned to the Worm Farm at midnight, carrying her lavish puncture repair kit, and made straight for the lab. Luckily, the searchlights were broken. She jimmied the door open with her spatula, and stepped inside. She could not risk turning the lights on, so she paused to allow her eyes to become accustomed to the darkness. When they had done so, she was nonplussed. The bicycles had vanished. In their place, a massive contraption of indeterminate purpose had been installed. At one point, the ceiling had been knocked through to make room for it. It took her a few moments to realise what had happened. The bicycles, or at least their constituent parts, were still there in the lab. They had been systematically taken to pieces and reassembled into this monstrous mechanism. She was unsure how to react. If she made overt investigations, or tampered with the contraption, her calumny would surely come to light. Yet how could she bear to abandon her scheme now, at so crucial a juncture? Tiptoeing from the lab, she crept away from the Worm Farm to ponder her dilemma.

TWELVE

She returned to the lab the following night. This time she brought with her a panoply of tools and mechanical bits and pieces capable of carrying out almost any technical reconstruction work she could think of. She had decided to take the purposeless contraption to pieces and to reassemble her bicycles one by one. It would not be possible to complete her task in a single night, but she had contingency plans. Demented violence was not beyond her. Nerve gas and dangerous chemical compounds were a language she understood. Before

Violetta

entering the lab, she made a detour to the squalid outbuildings on the edge of the Worm Farm and collected a few bags of cement, animal waste, and gritty particles. She had been awake all day plotting this escapade in fine detail, and left nothing to chance. Stowing the sacks by the porch, she entered the lab as before. Again she was nonplussed. This time the contraption itself had vanished. All trace of her broken bicycles was gone.

The hole in the ceiling had been repaired in a rudimentary fashion with rush matting. She spent four hours searching the entire premises, until dawn. She found nothing.

THIRTEEN

Her Sawtooth jet, with its delicate nubs and extra-sensitive roseate bellerophon system, circled low over the Worm Farm. Bleeping monitors in the cockpit recorded triggered-signal-delay codes and converted them into a veritable broth of gobbledegook which she would later be able to decipher at the Potato Building. The scanners picked up something lascivious and untoward from the Worm Farm Chaplaincy. She steered the plane around and swooped in low once more. Below, she could see Hellhound skirting the perimeter fence, a wooden carving of a swordfish tucked under his arm. She had grounds for suspecting that he was the man who had tampered with her bicycles. On impulse, she decided to strafe him. Setting the controls to automatic, she climbed up into the gun turret. Just as she was about to let loose a volley of lethal gunfire, the jet nosedived unaccountably and plunged into a lake. She was lucky to escape with her life.

FOURTEEN

Assuming the sallow urchin disguise took about an hour. In an anteroom within the Potato Building, she greased her hair down, applied flour and a yellow waxy substance to her face, and donned the greyish-brown rags. Their stench repelled her, but the deceit was necessary. Once the disguise was complete, with a steel rod shoved down one trouser leg, she practised her drool in front of the mirror and gave her greasy forelock a few experimental tugs. Perfect. Lurching urchin-like to Hellhound's office, she snivelled and hung her head. As expected, he summoned her at once. 'There you are, young fellow-me-lad! Go and get me some mountaineering pitons this instant!' She had grown used to his despotic manner and, bowing her head, made as if to scamper off in self-abasing fashion. As soon as she was out of the door, she heard Hellhound pick up the phone and dial. She waited, listening intently. She heard only snatches of his conversation. '. . . Another swingeing attack . . . bauxite . . . clumps of hay . . . destitution . . . ears . . . febrifuge . . . gin and blood oranges . . . halitosis . . . impermanence . . . Judgement Day . . . kept hooting . . . lavatorial . . . mishmash . . . no drudge worth their salt . . . obeisance . . . pestilential . . . Quisling-mouthed flibbertigibbet . . . rented socks . . . smudged . . . turnip soup . . . ungodly . . . viler by the minute . . . whisks . . . x-rays are not hollyhocks . . . you curmudgeonly swine . . . zoo-brain . . .' Pah! He was on the phone to that Elderberry wretch again, obviously. She made a low huffing sound and set off for the warehouse. As she crossed the grit circles, she stopped in her tracks. Perhaps Elderberry was an accomplice in the heinous mutilation of her bicycles! Tearing off her greasy wig and wrenching the steel rod out of her trouser leg, she turned around and pelted back to the Potato Building. Strictly speaking it was not part of the Worm Farm, but it had been annexed to it and the big fence enclosed it within the precincts. Panting, she threw open the doors. The monitors were bleeping away happily to themselves. She sat down at the Wesniod console, frantically tapping measured cross-referencing data into the wafery information banks, all the while throwing switches, adjusting the intricate system of pulleys, and fair wrenching the red sarcophagus levers off of their pointy hinges. At last her work was complete. A blip! indicated that the enormous printer was about to chug out the results. Smoking desperately, she waited to see what malevolence would be brought to light.

FIFTEEN

She clambered on to the roof of the latrine. The canisters were still there, but the pods had been disturbed. That much was obvious. A heron stood preening on the horizon, silhouetted against the setting sun. Where was Hellhound?

PART FOUR: VISITS SIXTEEN TO TWENTY

SIXTEEN

He tugged at the piece of string, and heard distant clanking. So far so good. That would be enough for one day. Replacing the iron helmet on his head, he fixed the bolts back into place and let dangle a delicate ribbon over the opening, as a safeguard. Sighing, he started up the huge granite staircase, holding carefully to the rail. The battery on his torch was running low. Wheezing, he finally reached the top. He squeezed past the rusted portcullis and whacked the tin tray set into the wall. There was a whirring noise, and the fine grille and plastic covering shifted to the left. He emerged into the light, and found himself standing ten yards away from Canute Hellhound. The Director of Research greeted him with a grim and gritty smile. The pair shook hands.

SEVENTEEN

Elderberry's canonisation was not unexpected. Three popes had testified to being spiritually uplifted by his Collected Sermons, and a small religious publishing house continued to issue his Diaries, with their fanatic itemisation of acts of charity and compassion, on a regular basis. Some felt that his alleged self-seeking character would disqualify him for the sainthood while still living, but the new pope had scotched these rumours in the most decisive manner. Elderberry's name was now ensconced firmly in the list of saints, between St. Egwin and St. Elias. It had been at his own suggestion that he had been officially proclaimed the Patron Saint of Worms; which was a partial explanation for his now daily visits to the Worm Farm. Here he would sprinkle holy water from the sacred wells at Coctlosh on any worm whose path he happened to cross, and offer devotional prayers in the Worm Farm Chaplaincy at noon each day. Canute Hellhound had issued a memorandum to the effect that any member of staff not attending these services, nor essaying the prayers with sufficient gusto and breast-beating, would be dismissed instantly, never to sully the Worm Farm with their heathen presence for ever more. Elderberry's evangelical enthusiasm was truly infectious; members of staff were forever volunteering new ways to pay obeisance to the patron saint. Huge trays of worms were carried bodily into the daily service, that they too might benefit from the light of faith shed incandescently about. Lavish floral decorations were hung from the entrance gates. Small plaster statuettes of Elderberry, decked out archaically in robes and tunics, were manufactured for sale in the Worm Farm Souvenir Shop. And yet there was a more sinister purpose to the saint's daily visitations. He and Hellhound were colluding in a project of no mean dimensions, destined to shake the world.

EIGHTEEN

Two days later, Elderberry again drove to a deserted spot some three miles away from the Worm Farm, and parked his car under a shelter of wild foliage and greenery. Whacking a tin tray set into the ground, he made entrance to a fabulous network of tunnels weaving for miles below the surface. One route took him to the wells at Coctlosh; one to his turnip patch; yet another to the dank cellars beneath the Worm Farm. It

Elderberry

was along this third tunnel that Elderberry repaired, dragging along behind him the infernal machine made out of whisks which, he hoped, would bring him another step closer to the accomplishment of his grand design.

NINETEEN

Violetta, returning a tray of worms to its rightful abode in Alpha Blue Wormery, saw Elderberry limping decisively towards the outbuildings. Foisting the tray upon a grizzled accomplice, she made to follow him, simultaneously setting the controls on her portable Arcane Hooter. This would transmit anything important back to the bleeping consoles in the Potato Building. Elderberry's frayed grey cassock billowed behind him in the wind. Snow was forecast, but had not yet fallen. He entered the most sordid of the huts and, after various complicated adjustments to a series of occult mechanisms concealed behind a pile of rotting turnips, began the long trudge down the granite staircase to the cellars. As the trapdoor clanged shut automatically behind him, he heard the muffled sound of the hut door creaking open on its hinges. Had he been followed? He had. Violetta stood in the stinking gloom, beflummoxed. She had seen Elderberry enter this hut, yet all trace of him had vanished. Dialling calculations on the Arcane Hooter, she listened out for the tiniest noise. Elderberry, a few feet underneath her, cursing that Hellhound had not yet installed adequate sound-proofing, tried to stifle the sound of his wheezing. Both remained like this for about a quarter of an hour, until it dawned on Violetta that her Arcane Hooter had been deliberately incapacitated. Her fury was demoniac. She smashed the hut to pieces in her rage, thereby unknowingly destroying Elderberry's entry and exit system. For this rank and vile hut housed the intricate network of technological mumbo-jumbo which controlled all the entrances to the cellars and their tributary tunnels. The Patron Saint of Worms was hopelessly trapped.

TWENTY

Covered in old sailcloth and sacking, Elderberry lay shivering in the dismal cellars, the fruits of years of impossibly brilliant

94

work stacked around him. The machine made of alabaster, the machine made of bicycles, the machine made of cork, the machine made of derailments . . . they were all here, splendid in their uselessness without the final one, the machine made of zaribas, which still lay in fragmentary bits of jumble in and around the turnip patch at the allotments. And now, trapped as he was, he had no way of collecting it, bringing it here to assume its place among the others. He would no longer be able to carry out the last and most crucial phase of the project, the majestic synthesis of the twenty six machines to create the Alphabet Monster, which would build a new heaven and a new earth.

PART FIVE: VISITS TWENTY ONE FORTY

Over the next year or so, I made desperate and repeated attempts to retrieve my bicycle. I think I must have visited the Worm Farm about twenty times in all. Eventually, on St. Elderberry's Day, I at last tracked down the woman who so long ago had promised to mend my trusty steed. I was roaming disconsolately around the very edge of the Worm Farm when I saw her, emerging from a sort of annexe building, carrying a massive crate. Upon being confronted, she poured out a sorry tale of such uncompromising stupidity that I had no choice but to believe it. Gracefully, she returned my soiled fiver. She then announced that she was leaving the Worm Farm to take up an appointment elsewhere. I don't know why she told me this. Apparently she was off to Greenland, to do some work involving ice, snow-ploughs and huskies. It seemed a bit of a change from worms, I thought. She explained that she felt very bitter about the past months at the Worm Farm, ever since Canute Hellhound had taken over as Director of Research. I remembered that I had once had an exciting conversation with this man on the subject of whisks. Bidding Violetta farewell and good luck, I walked over to Hellhound's office. It seemed to have suffered from fire damage. The man who made a half-hearted attempt at greeting me was but a shadow. No longer declaiming in vigorous terms about whisks, or anything else come to that, he sat slumped in a rickety metal chair, knocking back the best part of a bottle of hooch. There was a deadened look in his eyes, and he kept up a pathetic, dirge-like moaning all the time I remained with him. After a while, I realised that he was forming, albeit in broken and inarticulate fashion, the same two phrases over and over again: 'He's in heaven' and 'I'm not'. I tried to find out what in god's name he was going on about, but he met my enquiries with a stare of formidable vacancy. In the end I could bear it no longer. With an absurd display of affection, I patted him on the head and mussed his filthy hair. Then I left the Worm Farm for the last time. I caught the bus back to my allotment and spent the rest of the day in my shed, planning marvellous feats with root vegetables. It began to rain, and I looked across at the ruinous state of the turnip patch. I hadn't seen my neighbour since the day he gave me an abortive lift to the Worm Farm. I made a sudden decision to put his allotment back into good order. Eyeing the packets of turnip seeds on my shelf, I stood up, grabbed hold of my hoe, and walked out of the shed into the downpour.

ARAMINTA DITCH

John Lennon

ARAMINTA DITCH was always larfing. She woof larf at these, larf at thas. Always larfing she was. Many body peofle woof look atat her saying, 'Why does that Araminta Ditch keep larfing?' They could never understamp why she was ever larfing about the place. 'I hope she's not at all larfing at me,' some peokle would say, 'I certainly hope that Araminta Ditch is not larfing at me.'

One date Araminta rose up out of her duffle bed, larfing as usual with that insage larf peojle had come to know her form.

'Hee! hee! hee!' She larfed all the way down to breakfart.

'Hee! hee! hee!' She gurgled over the morman papiers.

'Hee! hee! hee!' Continude Araminta on the buzz to wirk.

This pubbled the passages and condoctor equally both. 'Why is that boot larfing all the time?' Inqueered an elderberry passengeorge who trabelled regularge on that roof and had a write to know.

'I bet nobody knows why I am always larfing,' said Araminta to herself privately, to herself. 'They would dearly love to know why I am always larfing like this to myselve privately to myself. I bet some peoble would really like to know.' She was right, off course, lots of peotle would.

Araminta Ditch had a boyfred who could never see the joke. 'As long as she's happy,' he said. He was a good man. 'Pray tell me, Araminta, why is it that you larf so readily. Yeaye, but I am sorly troubled sometimes when thy larfter causes sitch tribulation and embarresment amongst my family and elders.' Araminta would larf all the more at an outburp like this, even to the point of hysteriffs. 'Hee! hee! hee!' She would scream as if possesed by the very double himself.

'That Araminta Ditch will have to storp orl these larfing;

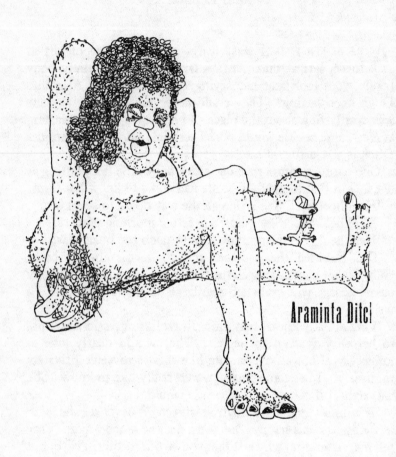

Araminta Ditc[

she will definitely have to storp it. I will go crazy if she don't storp it.' This was the large voice of her goodly neighbore, Mrs Cramsby, who lived right next door and looked after the cats whilst Araminta was at work. 'Takes a good deal of looking after these cat when she's at work – and that's nothing to larf about!'

The whole street had beginning to worry about Araminta's larfter. Why? hadn't she been larfing and living there for nye-bevan thirty years, continually larfing hee! hee! and annoying them? They began to hold meters to see what could be done – after all they had to live with her hadn't they? It was them who had to always keep hearing her inane larftor. At one such meetinge they deciple to call on the help of Araminta's boyfriend who was called Richard (sometimes Richard the Turd, but thats another story). 'Well I dont know dear friends,' said Richard, who hated them all. This was at the second meetink!

Obvouslieg samting hed tow be doon – and quickly. Araminta's face was spreading aboon the country, peochle fram all walks of leg began to regarden her with a certain insight left.

'What canon I do that would quell this mirth what is gradually drying me to drink, have I not bespoken to her often, betting her to cease, threatling – cajolson – arsking, pleases stop this larftor Araminta. I am at the end of my leather – my cup kenneth conner,' Richard say. The people of the street mubbered in agreement, what could he do? He was foing his vest. 'We will ask the Vicar,' said Mrs Crambsy, 'Surely he can exercise it out of her?' The peodle agreed – 'Surely the Vicar can do it if anybotty can.' The Vicar smiled a funny little smile wholst the goo people splained the troumer. When they had had finished speaching he rose up grandly from his barthchair and said loud and clear 'What do you mean exactly?' The peodle sighed an slowlies started to start again telling him about the awful case of Araminta's larfing.

'You mean she just keeps larfing fer no a parent season?' he said brightly. 'Yess that's it fazackerly Vicar,' said Richard, 'morning noon and nige, always larfing like a mad thin.' The Vicar looked up from his knitting and opened his mouths.

'Something will have to be done about that girl larfing all the time. It's not right.'

'I really doughnut see that it is any concervative of thiers whether i larf or nament,' sighed Araminta over a lengthy victim. 'The trifle with the peomle around here is that they have forgoden how, I repeat, how to larf, reverend, that's what I think anyhow.'

She was of corset talking to the extremely reverend LIONEL HUGHES. She had gone to see him in case he could help her in any small way, considering he was always spouting off about helping peouple she thought she'd give him a try as it were. 'What can I say my dear, I mean what can I say?' Araminta looked at the holy fink with disbelief. 'What do you mean – what can I say – don't ask me what to say. I cam here to ask you for help and you have the audacidacidity to ask me what to say – is that all you have to say?' she yellowed. 'I know exactly how you feel Samantha, I had a cousin the same way, couldn't see a thin without his glasgows.'

Araminta stood up in a kind of suit, she picked up her own mongels and ran seriously out of the room. 'No wonder he only gets three in on Sunday!' she exclaimed to a small group of wellwishers.

A year or more passedover with no changei in Araminta's strange larfing. 'Hee! hee! hee!' she went drivan herself and everone around her insane. THERE SEEMED NO END TO THE PROBLEM. This went on for eighty years until Araminta died larfing. This did not help her neighbers much. They had all died first, – which was one of the many things that Araminta died larfing off.

THE CHILDREN'S MARQUIS DE SADE

Marcel Marien

T HERE ONCE WAS a fairy whose name was Juliette. She was gentle, graceful, and beautiful, and they called her also the Apple Fairy, after the two apples she always wore on her chest. These apples were round and smelled good and she offered them to all who asked to be able to roll them over their tongues. Now, although everyone bit into them, they were nevertheless always full and whole and of perfect shape.

In the same country where the fairy lived, there was also an ogre who was called Saint-Fond. He was a horrible nasty, who sowed desolation wherever he happened to go. He was armed with a big dagger fourteen and a half inches long that he wore attached to his body and this was the instrument with which he perpetrated his horrible heinous crimes. This dagger was magic. The ogre by the way had been good, and would have remained so if, when he was seven, while he was still only a little boy, a wicked fairy who had the name of Nature had not cast a spell over him in the form of this dagger, which she had joined so skillfully to his lower abdomen that it was no longer possible to detach it. And so, inseparable from this treacherous weapon, the little boy grew and became in spite of himself the terrible ogre who brought sadness to the countryside.

But many other marvels were told of this dagger. How, for example, when it was not in use it was limp and soft, as if it were nothing but the sheath of skin enclosing it. But every time a victim came before the ogre, the terrible dagger would swell hugely, until it burst through the end of the sheath, and then it stood up with such energy that it irresistibly carried along the ogre, born good, who thus had to participate willy-nilly in the evil deeds his magic weapon compelled him to carry out.

One fine summer's afternoon, the sweet fairy Juliette was

out gathering flowers in a meadow when, suddenly, she found herself face to face with the horrible Saint-Fond. No sooner had they caught sight of one another than the dagger swelled beyond measure, leveled at the fairy. It was thick and red, and you'd have thought it was from perpetually gorging itself on blood that it took that fine scarlet shade making it only the more terrible to see. But Juliette was not afraid and, instead of running away, she approached the monster and started to laugh. 'Look, your lordship,' she then said, pulling up her dress. And by a magic effect she made a fresh wound appear on her body. 'Why then would you wish to wound me, since I am wounded already?' And with her delicate fingers, Juliette separated the edges of the wound just a little, as if to show that it was indeed real. And the ogre could see that the inside of the wound was pink and very deep. But the magic dagger was not the least bit abashed. It charged at Juliette, carrying the poor ogre along with it, and it had no sooner thrown the good fairy down on the grass than it began to dig into the marvelous wound furiously, plunging in up to the hilt.

After a moment the dagger came out again but as it wanted to drive itself elsewhere into the fairy's flesh, immediately at that very spot, anticipating its penetration, a new wound appeared, into which the sightless weapon thrust in a frenzy. During this time Juliette, who was staring into the eyes of the ogre bending over her, recognized deep in them the gentle glance of the man who had been born good and she felt great compassion for him. She held out to him one after the other the apples she wore on her chest and forced the ogre to taste them. He nibbled them gently, so that the fairy was moved to tears. With a lithe, adroit movement she rid herself of the dagger bruising her and knelt at the ogre's feet, forcing him to get up. Courageously, then, she brought her little mouth to the terrible dagger and although the latter was of enormous proportions, she succeeded in taking it in, letting it slide gently between her lips. After a moment, and without her attitude giving any warning of this, while the dagger was thrust so far into the back of her throat that she almost gagged, Juliette, suddenly bringing her teeth together, bit off the magic dagger level with the belly and briskly spat it out on the ground. At once the monstrous weapon could be seen, as though taken with convulsions, wriggling the way a snake does, growing quiet, and finally changing to stone.

Freed of his abominable instrument, Saint-Fond was no longer an ogre. He had become a good man once more. And so he was able to marry the fairy, but, a curious thing, they had no children.

MY DEAR HOW DEAD YOU LOOK
AND YET YOU SWEETLY SING

Priscilla Marron

FLORENCE under the floorboards did wonders for Wilbraham.

Made a new man of him. Shed several years he did. Lighthearted laughing days again he knew.

Wasn't going to caper off like Crippen. Not mad about male impersonators. No rage for the rolling deep.

Tap dance over her tomb he did. Delight fandango. Lissom as an agile lad.

Came, however, uncomfortable evenings. Songs by sad deceased. Visible in various sections. A wife in slices sings.

Haunting contralto she had. Real eerie. Sang better than Wilbraham danced she did. Cause connubial envy that can. Killing thing for vocally out-voxed fandango flinger. Hence histrionic hacksaw. Planks of heartfelt thanks. Sorry, Florrie. So long, Flo.

> *You mustn't imagine it's dead I am*
> *Though it's sitting without my head I am,*

sang Florence.

Wilbraham wasn't liking it one bit.

> *You mustn't imagine it's drunk I am*
> *Though it's warbling without my trunk I am,*

sang Florence.

Enthusiastic Wilbraham wasn't in the least.

> *You mustn't imagine it's nuts I am*
> *Though it's knifing you through the guts I am,*

Florence charmingly carolled.

Wilbraham wasn't even listening any more.

Neighbours got nosy. Called cops. Wilbraham wantonly extinct. Hatpin through heart.

Florence *uxor intacta* under floorboards. No parts peculiarly missing. Songless. Hand sticking up though. Second hatpin in it. Poised for posthumous assault.

Sad moral story. Stick to divorce court. Take no hacksaw to your *hausfrau*. Direct route too drastic.

Employ intermediary. Practise do-it-yourself by proxy. Eschew fatal fretwork.

You'll be stronger longer the fewer you skewer with that gnat bat the matrimonial wife knife. Fact exact!

JUST WHAT PURPOSE DO WHITE DOG STOOLS ACTUALLY SERVE?

Gustav Merink

'Rally to the Fatherland,
Our dear, dear Fatherland.'

ONLY VERY FEW people realise that they serve any purpose whatsoever. But they do quite definitely serve a very special purpose, there can be no doubt about it.

Every day, when I leave my house in the early morning, shortly before the postman arrives and shoves a heap of paper in my letterbox – which is anyhow fitted with a water flush, I stop for a moment in my garden and say out loud: Ksss Ksss.

And at once a highly bewildering phenomenon is initiated. A buzzing, coughing noise rises up out of the dead leaves on the ground, along with a scratching and a rustling snarl; two burning eyes start to glow at ankle height, and directly afterwards a black something or other, with a hairless encysted tumour on its neck, comes flying at me from behind the bushes and, seized by a mad rage, endeavours to bite the creases out of my trousers.

As yet I have been unable to establish to which order of beings the creature belongs.

It spends the morning hours crouching under an elder tree, its back humped. That's quite certain, I have found that much out little by little.

The maid swears that the phenomenon sometimes wears a blue coat lined in fire red and adorned with a crown at one corner. I was never able to perceive anything of the sort – despite the keenness of my observations – and it seems almost as if in this case the human retina acts differently from person to person.

Now whatever this creature with the encysted tumour may be, whether (going by the crown) it is the restless shade of the last degenerate scion of an extinct ruling house which assumes form under particular astrological aspects, or perhaps just a mere citizen of the animal kingdom, there is in any case something spectral about it which make me persist in my reservations concerning its materiality.

I sense quite clearly that it is very, very ancient, and I do not doubt that remembering the battle of Cannae* must be a piece of cake for it, for the scent of antiquity lingers about it!

But for all its grey-beardedness there is nothing mellow about it; its heart is filled with hatred for a whole world.

As yet it has failed to actually bite my trouser creases. This also lends weight to the argument that we could be dealing with a reflection from another sphere! For every time some imponderable, invisible force seems to compel it to leave off at the last fraction of a second, even though it never wearies of its efforts and continually starts anew.

The phenomenon ceases as abruptly as it begins.

That is to say a piercing voice suddenly descends from the heavens, without any warning, and calls:

Ah— —miii! Ah— —miii!

Quite distinctly: Ah— —miii!

I don't find anything remarkable about this. How often did a voice call out from the heavens to the ancient Jews for example? So why not for me, here in Columbus Lane . . .?

However, the voice has a devastating effect on the creature with the encysted tumour.

With a start the phantom leaves off of me and like a bolt of lightning it scrambles under the garden gate and races round the corner where it instantly . . . dematerialises!

It seems that the word 'Ah— —miii' is one of those abominable alliterative formulae which one finds hinted at in the Lamrim of the Tson-ka-pa, the fearful Tibetan books of conjuration. When spoken correctly they are able to release astral whirlwinds on the plane of causation that are so powerful that even we, clad in our protective shells of matter, perceive the final ramifications of such catastrophes in the form of inexplicable spectral occurences.

I have often chanted the mysterious syllables 'Ah— —miii' myself! At first with trepidation, then ever more courageously, but a visible change in the world of matter has never occurred.

Presumably my intonation was incorrect.

Or is its effectiveness dependent on a previously strict asceticism on the chanter's part?

The process which I witness every morning is by no means finished when the being with the encysted tumour dematerialises.

For scarcely has the heavenly voice faded than a disabled soldier enters the garden and silently approaches the elder tree.

I never trust transitory appearances – the senses are particularly poor guarantors of abstract knowledge – but the disabled soldier is certainly real. I have had him photographed.

The old warrior removes a few pale objects[1] from the earth with a coal rake – and triumphantly casts them to the others in the half full sack which he carries on his right shoulder as a counter-weight – the left being decorated with medals for bravery.

There is something diabolic about the fact that the pale objects always lie on exactly the same spot which the being with the encysted tumour had left shortly before . . . !

Without a doubt, there is an eery connection here!

If just any old pauper were to collect the pale objects the matter would hardly be worthy of comment. One must remember, they possess only a slight value, apparently serving some very minor function in Nature's metabolism. But here!?

Disabled soldiers collect the likes of them?!

Does not the Fatherland open both hands and bestow honour and riches on these men, in solemn remembrance of

---

[1]Without doubt, white dog excrement.

its debt of gratitude for their spilt blood and sacrificed limbs?

What are they doing hunting around for filth!?

There's a false bottom to this matter!!!

Naturally there will be hosts of alarmists who will once again try to argue that disabled soldiers are poor. But their evil intentions are more than transparent. It's completely obvious that – should the Fatherland really have failed this one time – the Kaiser himself would jump in with a joyous heart. For indeed, the spirit of sacrifice for the Fatherland, to which our 'true' poets. have always warmly recommended we should rally, does not go unrewarded.

So there must be something very special about these pale objects! Admittedly I reached this insight ages ago. One morning I read in the paper that an aged, one-legged veteran of the Italian Campaign had been found dead in a small room with no other possessions than a coal rake and – a sack full of white dog excrement, it hit me like an electric shock, as if an evil compulsion was now forcing me to investigate this riddle to the very end. Yet another disabled soldier! Yet again, that sack! And what had become of the piled up riches of the deceased? Eh?

He must have thought very little of them, he must have thought: 'What are they to me, so long as I have my sack.'

I remembered the story of the dervish from the Thousand and One Nights, the one who, having broken into the treasure store, paid no attention to all the treasures and merely took a small pot of ointment which, anointing the eyes, promised power over the entire world.

I realized that an incredible value – the key to untold pleasures – must be hidden within these pale objects if disabled soldiers, of all people, – those moody, molly-coddled favourites of the nation – were prepared to rummage around, leaving no stone unturned and cocking a snoop at every inclemency of the weather, in order to gain possession of them.

I went straight to the police. The coal rake was still there. But the sack . . . there was no trace!! And no one knew what had become of it! . . . As I thought!

Obviously someone or other had staked everything to get hold of it! At the last moment snatched it with unbelievable daring from the very jaws of the police! And just what purpose do white dog stools serve, I asked myself, 'what is their purpose?'

I looked in my encyclopaedia under D, under E, under W, under S – in vain.

It would have been ridiculous to question my disabled soldier. He would be the last to reveal the secret. So I wrote to the Ministry of Public Instruction.

I received no answer!

I went to a lecture given by a famous speaker and when the public was invited to write their questions on slips of paper, I also handed in mine. But as it came into his hands, he screwed it up and left the hall in indignation.

I could not find the office responsible at the town hall and was not admitted to see the mayor.

'You stick them on the ceiling in staterooms and then its called "stucco",' a cynic scoffed.

'They are the pathos among their kind, they are their own end,' the poet Peter Altenberg opined dreamily.

On the other hand an eminent scholar became frosty and off-hand, sternly replying: 'Such matters should not pass one's lips in polite company. Incidentally, they are the first signs of grave digestive disorders and their purpose (and with this word his eyes flashed with reproach), their purpose, is to warn the well-to-do layman never to arrange his life without the advice of an experienced doctor!' On the other hand, a man of the people said nothing at all, just boxed my ears without a word . . .!

I tried a different approach, I went up to people on the street who possessed a mysterious appearance and posed my question bluntly. Hoping to catch them out. Short and direct, without beating about the bush.

They started back in dismay and fled with every indication of terror!

Then I resolved to delve into the depths of this mystery on my own and, deciding to perform chemical experiments, I set out in search of the substance myself.

As if some dark power were mocking me, the spot beneath the elder tree remained empty for days on end, and – strangely – the being with the encysted tumour also seemed to have disappeared.

I cannot even think of it without a feeling of horror.

For a whole week I searched along derelict walls and did not overlook a single monument. All in vain! And when fortune at last smiled on me and I had acquired the object of my longings and secreted it in a phial, I was suddenly beset by an excruciating fear. What if I were suddenly to fall in a faint right here on the spot, or even be seized by a stroke!? The substance would be found on my person, people would say: 'He had a bad soul, was a pervert through and through, the swine.' . . . And my family's happiness would be banished once and for all! Yes and officers, to whom I am attached by an unbreakable tie of the warmest affection, would turn up their noses and say: 'We knew it all along, he was an individualist!'

And the Young Men's Evangelical Association would fold its arms and dance an improving Protestant fandango on my grave.

I threw the phial away, as far as I could.

The next thing I plunged into was the study of the history of secret societies. There cannot be a brotherhood still in existence which I did not join, and doubtlessly were I to give all the profound signals of recognition and emergency which I have at my disposal one after another, I would be bundled off to a mad house as a suspected case of St. Vitus Dance.

But I won't give up.

I must find out what 'its' purpose is.

Every fibre in me shouts that there is a dread Order, a silent association of people for whom every door is open and who, immune to the arrows of chance, lead the world by the nose. They hold sway over every power in the world and use it to celebrate the most horrifying orgies, unpunished!

What were the Stercatorites of the Middle Ages, who bragged that they alone among the alchemists possessed the 'material,' other than confessors of this sect?

The age-old forgotten order of 'Pugs,' what other aim could they have had?

And the tentacles of these 'brothers' reach right into our own times!

Who is their chief? Where is the centre point around which they collect?

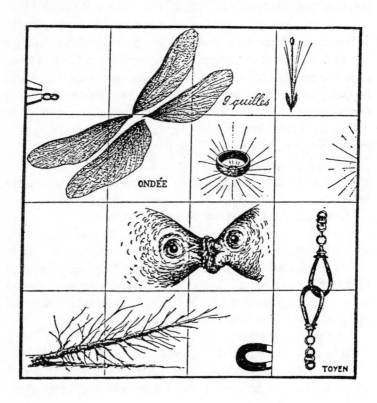

I suspect that the sinister Ohlendorff, Hamburg's un-crowned guano king, must have been their last Grand Master; but who is it now . . .?

Oh! Who rules over these disabled soldiers!

They will pile treasure upon treasure with their coal rakes and then . . . woe betide us all.

I look into the future with foreboding.

The days pass by, and none of them brings me the answer to my question: what purpose do 'they' actually serve?

And the night fades into dawn, the cock cries anxiously for the tardy day, I lie still awake in my bed, while outside the phantom with the encysted tumour is perhaps already in action beneath the elder tree.

Still half dreaming I see the figures of the disabled soldiers proceeding in their legions to The Brocken*, radiant in their precious gems. And I toss and turn in torment, sighing and groaning: what, yes, just what purpose do white dog stools actually serve!?

AUTHOR'S AFTERWORD: I am not interested in receiving elucidatory letters from the public claiming that the mysterious substance is employed in the tanning of leather gloves.

FROM HAND TO MOUTH

Fitz-James O'Brien

'The single most striking example of surrealistic fiction to precede *Alice in Wonderland*' was written as a serial story for *The New York Picayune* in 1858, and has scarcely been seen since. Its author holds a key place in the development of the American short story, bridging the gap between Poe and Bierce, and he is especially highly regarded in science fiction and fantasy circles, where stories like 'The Diamond Lens' and 'What Was It?' are frequently reprinted. 'From Hand to Mouth', a truly extraordinary tale, is a real discovery for lovers of bizarre humor – though O'Brien did not complete the tale: the last instalment, which offers an extremely lame ending, was supplied by the editor of the *Picayune* in the belief that the story had got so far out of hand that it was out of control.

I / HOW I FELL IN WITH COUNT GOLOPTIOUS

THE EVENING OF the 8th of November, in the present year, was distinguished by the occurrence of two sufficiently remarkable events. On that evening Mr. Ullman produced Meyerbeer's opera of 'The Huguenots', for the first time in this country, and we were unexpectedly visited by a snowstorm. Winter and the great lyrical dramatist made their debut together. Winter opened with a slow movement of heavy snowflakes, – an andante, soft and melancholy, and breathing of polar drowsiness. The echoing streets were muffled, and the racket and din of thoroughfares sounded like the roar of a far-off ocean. The large flakes fell sleepily through the dim blue air, like soft white birds that had been stricken with cold in the upper skies, and were sinking benumbed to earth. The trees and lamp-posts, decorated with snowy powder, gave the city the air of being laid out for a grand supper-party, with ornamental confectionery embellishing the long white table. Through the hoar drifts that lay along the streets peeped the black tips of building-stones and mud-piles in front of half-finished houses, until Broadway looked as if it was enveloped in an ermine robe, dotted with the black tails with which cunning furriers ornament that skin.

Despite the snow, I sallied forth with my friend Cobra, the musical critic of the New York *Daily Cockchafer*, to hear Meyerbeer's masterpiece. We entered a mute omnibus with a frozen driver, whose congealed hands could scarcely close upon our faces – which accounted perhaps for a slight error in the change he gave us – and so rolled up silently to Union Square, whence we floundered into the Academy. I listened to that wonderful picture of one of France's anniversaries of massacre, with bloody copies of which that 'God-protected country' (*vide* speech from the throne on any public occasion) is continually furnishing the civilized world. The roar of Catholic cannon – the whistle of Huguenot bullets – the stealthy tread of conspiring priests – the mournful wailing of women whose hearts foretell evil before it comes – the sudden outburst of the treacherous, bloodthirsty Romish tiger – the flight and shrieks of men and women about to die – the valiant, despairing fighting of the stern Protestants – the voice of the devilish French king, shouting from his balcony to his assassins the remorseless command, 'Tuez! tuez!' – the ominous trickling of the red streams that sprung from cloven Lutheran hearts, and rolled slowly through the kennels: – all this arose before me vital and real, as the music of that somber opera smote the air. Cobra, whose business it was – being a critic – not to attend to the performance, languidly surveyed the house, or availed himself of the intermission between the acts to fortify himself with certain refreshing but stimulating beverages.

The opera being concluded, we proceeded to Pilgarlik's – Pilgarlik keeps a charming private restaurant at the upper end of Broadway – and there, over a few reed-birds and a bottle of Burgundy, Cobra concocted his criticism on 'The Huguenots,' – in which he talked learnedly of dominants, subdominants, ascending by thirds, and descending by twenty-thirds, and such like, while I, with nothing more weighty on my mind than paying for the supper, smoked my cigar and sipped my concluding cup of black coffee in a state of divine repose.

The snow was deep, when, at about one o'clock, A.M., Cobra and myself parted at the corner of Eighth Street and Broadway, each bound for his respective home. Cobra lived on Fourth Avenue – I live, or lived, on Bleecker Street. The snow was deep, and the city quite still, as I half ran, half floundered down the sidewalk, thinking what a nice hot brandy-toddy I would make myself when I got home, and the pleasure I would have in boiling the water over my gas-light on a lately invented apparatus which I had acquired, and in which I took much pride; I also recollected with a thrill of pleasure that I had purchased a fresh supply of lemons that morning, so that nothing was needed for the scientific concoction of a nightcap. I turned down Bleecker Street and reached my door. I was singing a snatch of Pierre Dupont's song of *La Vigne* as I pulled out my night-key and inserted it in that orifice so perplexing to young men who have been to a late supper. One vigorous twist, and I was at home. The half-uttered triumphal chant of the Frenchman, who dilates with metrical malice on the fact that the vine does not flourish in England, died on my lips. They key turned, but the door, usually so yielding to the members of our family, obstinately refused to open. A horrible thought flashed across my mind. They had locked me out! A new servant had perhaps arrived, and cautiously barricaded the entrance; or the landlady – to whom, at the moment, I was under some slight pecuniary responsibility – had taken this cruel means of recalling me to a sense of my position. But it could not be. There was some mistake. There was fluff in my key – yes, that was it – there was fluff in the barrel of my night-key. I instantly proceeded to make a Pandean pipe of that instrument, and blew into the tube until my face resembled that queer picture of the wind in Aesop's fables, as it is represented in the act of endeavoring to make the traveller take off his cloak. A hopelessly shrill sound responded to my efforts. The key was clear as a flute. Was it the wrong key? I felt in every pocket, vaguely expecting a supernumerary one to turn up, but in vain. While thus occupied, the conviction forced itself on my mind that I had no money.

Locked out, with a foot of snow on the ground, and nothing but a three-cent piece and two new cents – so painfully bright that they presented illusory resemblances to half-eagles – in my pocket!

I knew well that an appeal to the bell was hopeless. I had tried it once before for three hours at a stretch, without the slightest avail. It is my private conviction that every member of that household, who slept at all within hearing of the bell, carefully stuffed his or her ears with cotton before retiring for the night, so as to be out of the reach of temptation to answer it. Every inmate of that establishment, after a certain hour, determinedly rehearsed the part of Ulysses when he was passing the Sirens. They were deaf to the melody of the bell. I once knew a physician who, to keep up appearances, had a night-bell affixed to his door. The initiated alone knew that he regularly took the tongue out before he went to bed. His conscience was satisfied, and he slept calmly. I might just as well have been pulling his bell.

Break the windows! Why not? Excellent idea; but, as I before stated, my pecuniary position scarcely allowed of such liberties. What was I to do? I could not walk up and down the city all night. I would freeze to death, and there would be a horrible paragraph in the morning papers about the sad death of a destitute author. I ran over rapidly in my mind every hotel in the city with which I was at all acquainted, in order to see if there was in any one of them a night-porter who knew me. Alas! Night-porters knew me not. Why had I not a watch or a diamond ring? I resolved on the instant to purchase both as soon as I got ten or twelve hundred dollars. I began to wonder where the newsboys' depot was, and recollected there was a warm spot somewhere over the *Herald* press-room, on which I had seen ragged urchins huddling as I passed by late of night. I was ruminating gravely over the awful position in which I was placed, when a loud but somewhat buttery voice disturbed me by shouting from the sidewalk: 'Ha, ha! Capital joke! Locked out, eh? You'll never get in.'

A stranger! perhaps benevolent, thought I. If so, I am indeed saved. To rush down the steps, place my hand upon his shoulder, and gaze into his face with the most winning expression I was capable of assuming, was but the work of several minutes – which, however, included two tumbles on the stoop.

'Can it – can it be,' I said, 'that you have a night-key?'

'A night-key!' he answered with a jolly laugh, and speaking as if his mouth was full of turtle – 'a night-key! What the deuce should I do with a night-key? I never go home until morning.'

'Sir,' said I, sadly, 'do not jest with the misery of a fellow-creature. I conjure you by the sanctity of your fireside to lend me your night-key.'

'You've got one in your hand; why don't you use that?'

I had. In the excitement of the moment I had quite overlooked the fact that, if I had fifty night-keys, I would still have found myself on the wrong side of the door.

'The fact is – pardon me – but I forgot that the door was locked on the inside.'

'Well, you can't get in, and you can't stay out,' said the stranger, chuckling over a large mouthful of turtle. 'What are you going to do?'

'Heaven only knows, unless you are in a position to lend me a dollar, which, sir, I assure you, shall be returned in the morning.'

'Nonsense. I never lend money. But if you like, you shall come to my hotel and spend the night there, free of charge.'

'What hotel?'

'The Hotel de Coup d'Oeil, on Broadway.'

'I never heard of such an establishment.'

'Perhaps. Nevertheless, it is what is called a first-class hotel.'

'Well, but who are you, sir?' I inquired; for, in truth, my suspicions began to be slightly excited by this time. My interlocutor was rather a singular-looking person, as well as I could make out his features in the dusk. Middle height, broad shoulders, and a square, pale face, the upper part of which seemed literally covered with a pair of huge blue spectacles, while the lower portion was hidden in a frizzly beard. A small space on either cheek was all that was uncovered, and that shone white and cold as the snow that lay on the streets. 'Who are you, sir?'

'I – I am Count Goloptious, Literary Man, *Bon vivant*, Foreign Nobleman, Linguist, Duellist, Dramatist, and Philanthropist.'

'Rather contradictory pursuits, sir,' I said, rather puzzled by the man's manner, and wishing to say something.

'Of course. Every man is a mass of contradictions in his present social state.'

'But I never heard your name mentioned in the literary world,' I remarked. 'What have you written?'

'What have I not written? Gory essays upon Kansas for the New York *Tribune*. Smashing personal articles for the *Herald*. Carefully constructed noncommittal double-reflex-action with escape-movement leaders for the *Daily Times*; sensation dramas for the Phantom Theatre. Boisterous practical joke comedies for Mr. Behemoth the low comedian; and so on *ad infinitum*.'

'Then as a *bon vivant* –?'

'I have been immensely distinguished. When Brillat Savarin was in this country, I invented a dish which nearly killed him. I called it Surprise des Singes avec petite verole.'

'Linguist?'

'I speak seventeen languages, sir.'

'Duellist?'

'I was elected a Member of Congress for South Carolina.'

'Philanthropist?'

'Am I not offering to you, a stranger, the hospitality of the Hotel de Coup d'Oeil?'

'Enough, sir,' I cried; 'I accept your offer. I thank you for your timely assistance.'

'Then let us go,' answered the Count Goloptious, offering me his arm.

II / THE HOTEL DE COUP D'OEIL

The Count led me out of Bleecker Street into Broadway. We trudged a few blocks in silence, but whether towards Union Square or the Battery I could not for the life of me tell. It seemed as if I had lost all my old landmarks. The remarkable corners and signposts of the great thoroughfare seemed to have vanished.

We stopped at length before a large edifice, built of what seemed at first glance to be a species of variegated marble; on examining more closely, I perceived that every stone in the front of the building was a mosaic, in which was represented one of the four chief organs of the body. The stones were arranged in the form of a cross, with these designs depicted on them.

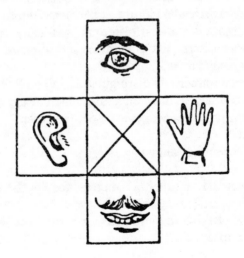

The effect of the entire front of this huge building, staring at you with a myriad painted eyes, listening to you with a myriad painted ears, beckoning to you with a myriad painted hands, and grinning at you with a myriad painted mouths, was inconceivably strange and bewildering.

'This is the hotel,' said Count Goloptious. 'Let us enter.'

We passed under a gigantic portal towards two gleaming doors of plate-glass, which voluntarily unclosed as we approached. A magnificent hall lay before us. The pavement was of tessellated marble, on every square of which the strange emblems which decorated the front of the establishment were repeated. From the center of this vast chamber a spiral staircase arose, from each coil of which small bridges of delicate gilt iron work branched off, and led into what seemed to be the corridors of the building. At one end of the hall stood a curious Oriental-looking structure, within which, seated upon a sort of throne, I beheld a portly bearded personage whose breast was festooned with gold chains, and whose fingers were covered with rings.

'That is the night clerk,' whispered the Count to me, pointing to this person. 'Go and enter your name on the book.'

I approached the Oriental temple, and, finding a hotel register with leaves of vellum and bound in silver and mother-of-pearl, open on a shelf close by, took up a pen and wrote down my name. The clerk did not even condescend to glance at me, while doing this.

'Would you like some supper?' asked the Count.

'No, no,' I answered; 'I want only to go to bed.' The truth is, the whole scene so bewildered me, that I began to fear that I had gone mad.

'Very well. I will call for your candle.' So saying the Count approached a large model of a human ear, which was fixed in the wall of the Oriental temple, and putting his lips to it called out, 'A bedroom light for 746.'

In an instant a continuous murmur seemed to fill the hall and ascend towards the roof of the building. It appeared to me that ten thousand voices took up the words, 'A bedroom light for 746,' one after the other, until the sentence rolled along like the fire of a line of infantry. I turned, startled, towards the direction from which those echoes proceeded, and on casting my eyes upon the great spiral staircase beheld the cause.

III / EYE, EAR, HAND, AND MOUTH

The balustrades of the staircase on either side, and the sides of the different galleries branching off, were all decorated with two of the mystical emblems I had before seen so often repeated in this strange hotel. On the one side a line of human mouths ran up the edges of the staircase, while on the other a line of human hands occupied a corresponding position. There was, however, this difference between them and the symbols occupying the front of the establishment. They were all modelled in high relief. The balustrades seemed as if they had been decorated with the pillage of numberless anatomical museums. As I turned suddenly and glanced towards the staircase, I saw the lips of those ten thousand mouths moving, and whispering softly but distinctly the words, 'A bedroom light for 746.'

I had scarcely recovered from the astonishment with which this sight overwhelmed me, and the rolling whisper had hardly died away in the domed roof of the hall, when my attention was attracted by a speck of light which appeared far away up on the staircase, and seemed to be travelling slowly down the huge spiral. I watched it with a sort of stupid interest, and when it came nearer discovered that it was nothing less than a chamber wax-light in a silver candlestick, which the ten thousand hands that lined the edge of the balustrade opposite to the balustrade of the mouths were carefully passing from one to the other. In a few moments it reached the bottom, where the last hand, a huge muscular-looking fist, held it.

'There is your light,' said the Count; 'follow it up stairs, and it will lead you to your room. I will, for the present, wish you a good-night, as I have to go and take my before-morning walk.'

I confusedly wished my strange friend good night, and walked towards the hand that held my candle. As I approached, the hand passed it to the hand next above, and the candle so began to ascend the stairs. I followed. After toiling up an interminable number of steps, the hands suddenly took the candle off into one of the side galleries, in which at last it stopped before a huge polished door, on the upper panels of which were painted again a huge eye and an equally gigantic ear. I could not help noticing that the eye had a demoniac expression.

I pushed the door open, and, taking the candle from the attendant hand, was about to enter the room, when my attention was attracted by that member giving my coat a gentle twitch. I turned, and there beheld the hand stretched out with an expression – if ever hand had an expression – which was inexpressibly pleading. I was puzzled. What could it want? I would follow the example of my friend Count Goloptious, and speak to the ear. Approaching my lips to the ear painted over my door, I put the question, 'What does this amiable hand want?' In an instant a fusillade of whispers came rolling up the line of mouths, answering, 'He wants a quarter for his trouble.' My heart sank – I had only five cents.

'Pshaw!' said I, trying to bluff the thing off, 'I can't attend to it now'; and so saying, stepped towards my room. As I entered and hurriedly closed the door, I beheld every hand down the long coil of stairs simultaneously double up and shake at me in menace, while a horrid sardonic laugh ran down the line of mouths. I never beheld anything more devilish than that spiral smile of scorn.

On closing the door of my room, I was not a little annoyed to find that the eye and the ear, which were on the outside, were on the inside also, so exactly alike that they seemed to have come through for the purpose of watching me, and listening to my sleep-talk. I felt wretchedly uncomfortable at the idea of undressing before that eye. It was fixed on me wherever I moved in the room. I tried to pin a handkerchief over it, but the wood of the door was too hard and the pins would not stick. As the handkerchief fell to the ground, I beheld the horrid eye wink at me with a devilish expression of derision. Determined not to be overlooked, I put out the light and undressed in the dark, when I tumbled into bed in a state of confusion of mind not easily described. I had scarcely laid my head on the pillow, when I heard a distinct knock at my door. Cursing the intrusion, and not without some tremor, being uncertain what new enchantment might be brewing, I opened it. There was the hand outstretched, and pleading for its infernal quarter. The abominable member was evidently determined to keep me awake all night. There was but one thing to be done – to bribe him with a promise. I put my lips to the ear and said: 'If the hand does not disturb me, I will put a gold ring on his finger tomorrow.'

The ten thousand mouths repeated with tones of approval, 'He will put a gold ring on his finger tomorrow,' and the ten thousand hands waved their thanks. I shut my door, congratulating myself on my escape, and, flinging myself on the bed, soon fell fast asleep.

IV / DR. KITCHENER IN A DREAM

A horrible heat seemed to surround my head. I suffered intolerable agony. Count Goloptious had unscrewed my caput just at the point known to anatomists as the condyles, and deliberately placed it in the center of a ring of burning brands which he had laid on the floor. The Philanthropic Duellist then drew a volume from his pocket, which, even in my excited condition, I could not help recognizing as Doctor Kitchener's cookery-book, and commenced deliberately to read aloud the recipe for roasting a goose alive, which is contained in that immortal work. I now perceived with unutterable indignation that he intended to cook my head after Kitchener's inhuman instructions.

The flames leaped higher and higher around my blistering cheeks. My whiskers – whiskers on which countless barbers had exhausted the resources of their art – shrivelled into ashy nothings. My eyeballs protruded, my lips cracked; my tongue, hard and wooden, beat against the roof of my mouth. I uttered a half-inarticulate cry for water. The Count laughed a devilish laugh, and consulted his book.

'True,' he said, 'the worthy doctor says, that when the goose thirsteth let her be fed with water, so that the flesh shall be tender when cooked. Let us give the poor head a drink.'

So saying, he reached towards my parched lips a pannikin fixed on the end of a long handle. I quaffed eagerly the liquor which it contained. Ah! how grateful was that draught of brandy-and-water! I drained the cup to the bottom. But the bliss was short-lived. The flames hissed and crackled. My hair caught fire, and my poor head blazed like a Frenchman's *'ponch-bol.'* The sparkles from the burning brands flew against my forehead and into my eyes, scorching and blinding me. My brain simmered in the arched cells of my skull. My anguish was insufferable, and as a last desperate resource I cried out to the Count: 'Take me from the fire – take me from the fire – I am overdone!'

The Count answered to this: 'Patience, patience, head of a heathen! You are roasting beautifully. A few minutes more, and I will pour some Worcestershire sauce over you.'

Worcestershire sauce! That essence of every peppery condiment known to civilized man! Worcestershire sauce, the delight of East Indian officers on half-pay, and the horror of Frenchmen who encounter it in London restaurants, and return to 'La Belle' with excoriated palates; this biting, inflammatory stuff to be poured over a wretched head, whose scalp was cracking like the skin of a roasted apple – it was too

much to endure, so I gave vent to my feelings in one unearthly shriek of agony and – awoke.

My head was hot, but, thank Heaven, it was not roasting. It was lying on a tumbled pillow across which a stream of the morning sunlight was pouring in a golden tide. There was no Count Goloptious – no circle of firebrands – no Worcestershire sauce – I was in bed, and alone in the Hotel de Coup d'Oeil.

So soon as I had sufficiently recovered from the effects of my horrible dream, I sat up in bed, and inspected my apartment. It was large and lofty and sumptuously furnished. A touching attention to my necessities was visible as I glanced round the room. By my bedside, on a small buhl table, stood a large tumbler containing a creaming champagne cocktail. I drained it as a libation to the God of Morning. It was an appropriate sacrifice. The early sunlight itself seemed to flash through its amber globules. The white foam of dawn creamed in its effervescence. The tonic flavor of the fresh air that blows over the awaking earth was represented by the few drops of Boker's bitters with which it was tinctured. The immediate glow which it sent through every limb typified the healthy circulation produced by morning exercise.

I lay back on my pillow and began to speculate on the strange series of incidents which had befallen me. Who was Count Goloptious? What weird hotel was this, of which I had become an inmate? Were the days of enchantment indeed revived? Or did I merely dream of that myriad of beseeching hands and whispering mouths and ever-wakeful eyes?

I glanced involuntarily to the door at this juncture, and lo! there I beheld the eye which seemed set in the panel of my door. A full flood of the sunlight that poured across my bed struck across that side of my room, and I saw the eye winking drowsily in the blaze – drowsily, but yet wakefully, like one who is accustomed to watch between sleeping and waking; a sentinel which was never entirely somnolent.

The eye was watching me, despite the sleepy film with which it was overspread. Did I make any abrupt movement in the bed, its half-closed lid suddenly opened, and stared at me with appalling vigilance. There was no avoiding it. It commanded every corner of the room.

How was I to rise and attire myself, with so unpleasant a supervision? I had no longer the resource of extinguishing the light. The sun was beyond the reach of such a process. I meditated for a while, and at length hit upon the idea of constructing a species of wigwam out of the bedclothes, and dressing myself under its shelter. This I accomplished all the more easily, as I had laid my clothes, on retiring to rest, within easy reach of the bed; and as I constructed my impromptu tent, I thought I could discern an expression of drowsy disappointment shooting from underneath the half-closed lid of the Sentinel Eye.

V / HOW I MAGNETIZED MY EYE

Having finished my toilet sufficiently to justify my stepping from my bed, I was proceeding with my ablutions, when I heard a few chords struck upon a piano, in what seemed to be the next apartment. The moment after, a rich, luxurious contralto voice commenced to sing Schubert's beautiful serenade. I listened entranced. It seemed as if Alboni herself were singing. Those showers of rich, round notes falling in rhythmical sequence; that *sostenuto*, that, when first uttered, seemed a sound too weak to live, but growing and swelling every moment until it filled all the air with delicious sound, and then lessening and lessening till it almost died away, like distant music heard across the sea at night; those firm accentuations; the precision of those vocal descents, when the voice seemed to leap from the pinnacles of the gamut with the surety and fearlessness of a chamois-hunter leaping from Alpine peaks – all told me that I was listening to a queen of song.

I ran to the window of my room, and, opening it, thrust my head forth. There was a window next to mine, but I could see nothing. The blinds were down, but I could feel the glass panes vibrating with that wondrous tide of song.

A woman – a great singer – the greatest I had ever heard, lived next to me. What was she like? That heavenly voice could never come from a lean and withered chest, from a skeleton throat. She must be young, must be lovely. I determined on the instant to form her acquaintance.

But there was the Sentinel Eye! How to evade the vigilance of that abominable optic? Its horrible magnetic gaze followed me in every motion that I made. Magnetic gaze! There was an idea. It was doubtless an enchanted eye; but was there any enchantment that could stand against the human will? I was strong, body and soul. My magnetic power I had frequently proved to be of the highest force; why not exercise it on my sentinel? I resolved to attempt to magnetize The Eye!

I shut the window, and, taking a chair, seated myself opposite the demoniac optic. I fixed my eyes upon it, and, concentrating all the will of which I was master, sent a powerful magnetic current straight to the center of the glaring pupil. It would be a desperate struggle, I knew, but I was determined not to succumb. The Eye became uneasy. It glanced hither and thither, and seemed to wish to avoid my gaze. The painted eyelids drooped; the devilish pupil contracted and dilated, but still the orb always had to return and meet mine.

Presently the glaze of a magnetic sleep began to overspread it. The scintillating lights that played within grew dim. The lid drooped, and, after lifting once or twice, I beheld the long, dark lashes fall, and slumber veiled my sentinel.

VI / FAIR ROSAMOND

No sooner was the Sentinel Eye fairly magnetized than I hastened to the window and flung it open. I possess a tolerable tenor voice, and as I thought vocalism was the simplest way of attracting the attention of the fair unknown, I sang the first verse of the charming serenade in the *Knight of Arva*; a melody full of grace and passion, for which Mr. Glover never obtained sufficient commendation. I had hardly concluded the first verse when I heard the neighboring window unclose. Unable to restrain my curiosity, I thrust my head out of my casement. Almost at the same instant a lovely face emerged from the window on the right. I had just time to get a flash of a glorious blond head, when the apparition disappeared. My head went in also. I waited a few moments, then cautiously, and after the manner of a turtle, protruded my caput once more. The Blond Head was out, but went in again like a flash. I remained with outstretched neck. After a brief pause I saw a gleam of fair curls. Then a white forehead, then a nose *retroussé*, then an entire face. I instantly withdrew into my shell. The Blond Head was timid, and I wished to encourage it.

Have you ever seen those philosophical toys which are constructed for the purpose of telling whether the day will be rainy or shiny? No. Then I will describe one to you.

There is a rustic house with two portals, one on either side. In the portal on the right a little man is concealed; in the portal on the left, a woman. They are both connected with a vertical coil of catgut, which runs from the base to the roof of the house, between the two. In dry weather the catgut relaxes, and the little man, by the action of such relaxation, is swung out of his portal into the open air. In wet weather the catgut contracts, and the woman enjoys the atmosphere. This toy has two advantages. One is, that it is infallible in its predictions, as it never announces fine weather until the weather is already fine; the other, that it affords an admirable illustration of the present social state of woman. When the day of storm arrives, in goes the man to his comfortable shelter, and out comes the woman to brave the elements. How many households does this typify! In sunshine and summer weather the husband is a charming fellow, and flaunts abroad in all his splendor; but when the clouds gather, when the fire goes out on the hearth for want of fuel, and duns are at the door, then poor woman is sent out to meet them, while the lord of creation hides in the cellar. I commend the toy to the consideration of Miss Lucy Stone.

Well, the Blond Head and myself played at weather-telling for five minutes. No sooner was one in than the other was out. It was a game of 'tee to – tottering' performed after a new fashion. I resolved to put an end to it.

I gave three distinct hems.

There is a good deal of expression in a 'hem.' There is the hem of alarm, such as Alexis gives to Corydon, who is flirting in the garden with Phillis, when that young lady's mother is approaching. There is the hem of importance, such as that with which old Beeswax, the merchant, who is 'worth his million, sir,' prefaces a remark: the hem of confusion – the hem of derision or unbelief – the hem of satisfaction – the hem of disappointment – in short, a whole circle or hemmysphere of hems, each expressive in its way of a peculiar emotion. My hem was the hem of interrogation.

It was answered, and the next moment the Blond Head hovered, as it were, on the window-sill. It looked like a bird whose cage door has been opened after years of captivity, and who flutters on the threshold, not daring to advance into the free air.

I advanced my head boldly, and caught the Blond Head on the wing. It was retreating after the usual fashion, and with the usual rapidity, when I shot it with the word –

'Stay!'

It fluttered for an instant, and then remained still.

'We are neighbors,' I remarked to the Blond Head. It was a truism, I know, but still it was a remark. After all, what does it matter what you say to most women, so that what you say is a remark?

'So I perceive,' answered the Head, still fluttering a little.

'May I have the honor of knowing –' I commenced.

'Certainly,' interrupted the Blond Head, 'I am Rosamond.

'The fair Rosamond, I see,' I interposed, in my gallantest manner.

'Yes,' replied Rosamond, with wonderful *naïveté*, 'fair perhaps, but very unhappy.'

'Unhappy! How? Can I relieve you – be of any service?'

A glance of suspicion was shot at me from a pair of large, lustrous blue eyes.

'Are you not one of his satellites?' asked the Blond Head.

'I a satellite?' I answered indignantly – 'I am no one's satellite – unless indeed it be yours,' I added; 'for I would gladly revolve round so fair a planet.'

'Then you are not a friend of Count Goloptious?'

'No. I never saw him until last night. He brought me to this hotel, where I have been bewildered by enchantments.'

'All my doing! all my doing!' cried Rosamond, wringing her hands.

'How your doing?' I inquired, with some astonishment.

'I am the artist – the fatal, the accursed artist. It was I who painted, I who modelled.'

'Painted, modelled what?'

'Hush! you can save me, perhaps. I will see you again today. Is not the Eye watching you?'

'I have magnetized it.'

'Good! you are a clever fellow,' and Rosamond's eyes sparkled. 'You must help me to escape.'

'From what?'

'I will tell you – but quick shut your window. Count Goloptious is coming.'

The Blond Head gave me a sweet smile, and retreated. I did likewise, and closed my window. The next moment my door opened, and Count Goloptious entered.

VII / THREE COLUMNS A DAY

Count Goloptious entered. He seemed somewhat agitated, and banged the door loudly. The shock dispelled the magnetic slumber of the Sentinel Eye, which suddenly opened its heavy lid and glared around with an expression which seemed to say, 'I'd like to catch anybody saying that I have been asleep!'

'Sir,' said the Count, 'you have been misconducting yourself.'

'I? Misconducting myself! What do you mean, Count Goloptious?'

'You have been singing love-songs, sir. In a tenor voice, too. If you were a bass I would not so much care, but to sing tenor – it's infamous!'

The blue goggles of the Count seemed to scintillate with anger as he glared at me.

'What the devil is the meaning of all this mystery?' I demanded angrily, for I really was getting savage at the incomprehensibility of everything that surrounded me. 'What do your infernal eyes and hands and ears and mouths mean? If you are a nightmare, why don't you say so, and let me wake up? Why can't I sing love-songs if I like – and in a tenor voice, if I like? I'll sing alto if I choose. Count Goloptious.'

'It is not for you to penetrate the mysteries of the Hotel de Coup d'Oeil, sir,' answered the Count. 'You have enjoyed its hospitalities, and you can go. You have sung tenor songs, sir. You know, as well as I, the influence of the tenor voice upon the female heart. You are familiar with the history of the opera, sir. You have beheld penniless Italians, with curled mustaches, and with no earthly attraction except a peculiar formation of the windpipe, wreck the peace of the loveliest of our females. There is a female in this vicinity, sir. A poor, weak-minded girl, who has been placed under my guardianship, and who is crazy on the subject of music. You have been singing to her, sir. Yes, with that accursed mellifluous voice of yours – that vocal honey in which you tenors administer the poison of your love – with that voice, sir, you are endeavoring to destroy the peace of mind of my ward. You have slept here, sir. You can go now.'

'I have not the slightest intention of going now, Count Goloptious. This hotel suits me admirably well. It has certain little drawbacks to be sure. It is not pleasant to be always overlooked and overheard in one's privacy.' Here I pointed to the Ear and the Eye. 'But still one can grow accustomed to that, I suppose. By the way, I should like some breakfast.'

My coolness took the Count completely by surprise. He stared at me without being able to utter a word. The fact was, that the Blond Head had bewitched me. Those clouds of golden hair that enfolded the wondrous oval of her face like a continual sunset had set my heart on fire. Never, never would I quit that hotel, unless I bore her with me. She had hinted at misfortune in our brief interview. She was a captive – a captive of the false Count, who now pretended that he was her guardian. Meshed in the countless spells and enchantments that surrounded her, she was helpless as those fair creatures we read of in the *Arabian Nights*. I would be her rescuer. I would discover the charm before which the bonds should melt. It was Andromache and Perseus and the sea-monster over again, in the year 1858. The Count, it is needless to say, was the monster. I had no Medusan shield, it is true, but I felt powerful as Perseus, for all that. My blond Andromache should be saved.

'So you won't go, eh?' said Goloptious, after a long silence.

'No.'

'You had better.'

'This is a hotel. I have a right to accommodation here as long as I pay for it. Hotels belong to the public, when the public has money.'

'I know I can't force you to go, but I don't think, young sir, that you will be able to pay for your board.'

'How much do you charge here, by the day?'

'Three columns a day.'

'Three what?'

'Three columns a day.'

'I have heard of pillar dollars, but hang me if I ever heard of money that was called columns.'

'We don't take money in pay at the Hotel de Coup d'Oeil. Brain is the only currency that passes here. You must write me three columns of the best literary matter every day; those are our terms for this room. We have rooms higher up which rent for less. Some go as low as a paragraph. This is a four-column room usually, but you can have it for three.'

Was the fellow laughing at me? His countenance was perfectly serious the whole time he was speaking. He talked as deliberately as if he had been a simple hotel clerk talking to a traveller, who was about pricing rooms. The whole thing struck me so comically that I could not refrain from a smile. I determined to carry the thing out in the Count's own vein.

'Meals are of course included?' I said inquiringly.

'Certainly, and served in your own room.'

'I don't think the apartment dear,' I continued, inspecting my chamber with a critical eye. 'I'll take it.'

'Very good'; and I saw a gleam of gratified malice shoot through the Count's great blue goggles.

'Now,' said I, 'perhaps you will inform me, Count Goloptious, why a few moments since you were so anxious to get rid of me, and why now you so tranquilly consent to my remaining an inmate of the Hotel de Coup d'Oeil?'

'I have my reasons,' said the Count, mysteriously. 'You have now taken a room in the Hotel de Coup d'Oeil; you will never quit it unless with my consent. The Eye shall watch you, the Ear shall hear you, the Hands shall detain you, the Mouths shall betray you; work is henceforth your portion. Your brain is my property; you shall spin it out as the spider his web, until you spin out your life with it. I have a lien on your intellect. There is one of my professions which I omitted in the catalogue which I gave you on our first meeting – I am a Publisher!'

VIII / THE BLOND HEAD

This last speech of the Count's, I confess, stunned me. He was then a publisher. I, who for years had been anxiously keeping my individuality as an author intact, who had been strenuously avoiding the vortex of the literary whirlpool of which the publisher is the center, who had resisted, successfully, the absorbing process by which that profession succeeds in sucking the vitals out of the literary man, now suddenly found myself on the outer edge of the maelstrom, slowly but surely revolving towards the central funnel which was to swallow me.

An anticipation of unknown misfortunes seemed to overwhelm me. There was something sternly prophetic in the last tones of Goloptious's voice. He seemed to have had no turtle in his throat for several days. He was harsh and strident.

I determined to consult with the Blond Head in my extremity. It would, at least, be a consolation to me to gaze into those wondrous blue eyes, to bask in the sunshine of that luminous hair.

I raised my window, and hummed a bar of *Com'e Gentil*. In a moment the adjoining window was raised, and out came the Blond Head. The likeness to the weather-toy existed no longer: both our heads were out together.

'You have seen Goloptious,' said the Blond Head. 'What did he say?'

'Excuse me from continuing the conversation just at this moment,' I replied. 'I have forgotten something.'

I had. The Ear and the Eye were in full play – one watching, the other listening. Such witnesses must be disposed of, if I was to hold any secret conversation with Rosamond. I retired therefore into my chamber again, and set to work to deliberately magnetize the eye. That organ did not seem to relish the operation at all, but it had no resource. In a few moments the film overspread it, and it closed. But what was to be done with the ear? I could not magnetize that. If, like the king in Hamlet, I had only a little poison to pour into it, I might deafen it forever. Or, like the sailors of Ulysses, when passing the island of the Sirens – ah! Ulysses! – that was the idea. Stop up the ear with wax! My bedroom candle was not all burned out. To appropriate a portion of that luminary, soften it in my hands, and plaster it over the auricular organ on my door was the work of a few moments. It was a triumph of strategy. Both my enchanted guardians completely entrapped, and by what simple means!

I now resumed my out-of-window conversation with Rosamond with a feeling of perfect security.

'I have seen Goloptious,' I said, in reply to her previous question, 'and am now a boarder in the Hotel de Coup d'Oeil.'

'Great heavens, then you are lost!' exclaimed Rosamond, shaking her cloudy curls at me.

'Lost! How so?'

'Simply that you are the slave of Goloptious. He will live on your brains, until every fiber is dried up. You will become a mental atrophy – and, alas! worse.'

'What do you mean? Explain, for Heaven's sake. You mystify me.'

'I cannot explain. But we must endeavor to escape. You are ingenious and bold. I saw that by the manner in which you overcame the Sentinel Eye by magnetism. This hotel is a den of enchantments. I have been confined here for over a year. My profession is that of a sculptor, and I have been forced to model all those demon hands and mouths and ears with which the building is so thickly sown. Those weird glances that strike through the countless corridors from the myriad eyes are of my painting. Those ten thousand lips that fill this place with unearthly murmurs are born of my fingers. It is I, who, under the relentless sway of Goloptious, have erected those enchanted symbols of which you are the victim. I knew not what I did, when I made those things. But you can evade them all. We can escape, if you will only set your ingenuity to work.'

'But, really, I see nothing to prevent our walking down stairs.'

'There is everything. You cannot move in this house without each motion being telegraphed. The Hands that line the staircase would clutch your skirts and hold you firm prisoner, were you to attempt to leave.'

'The Hands be – dished!' I exclaimed.

At this moment there came a knock. I hastily drew my head in, and opened my door. I beheld the Hand of the night before, pleadingly extended; and at the same moment a running fire of murmurs from the Mouths informed me that he wanted the gold ring I had promised him. It was evident that this infernal hand would dun me to all eternity, unless he was paid.

I rushed to the window in my despair.

'Rosamond! fair Rosamond!' I shouted. 'Have you got a gold ring?'

'Certainly,' answered the Blond Head, appearing.

'Stretch as far as you can out of your window and hand it to me.'

'Alas, I cannot stretch out of the window.'

'Why not?'

'Do not ask me – oh! do not ask me,' answered the Blond Head, with so much anguish in her tones that I inwardly cursed myself for putting so beautiful a creature to pain.

'But,' I continued, 'if I reach over to you with a pair of tongs, will you give it to me?'

'O, with pleasure!' and the Blond Head smiled a seraphic smile.

A pair of tongs being adjacent, a plain gold ring was quickly transferred from Rosamond's slender finger to my hand. With much ceremony I proceeded to place it on the smallest finger of the Hand, not being able, however, to get it farther than the first joint. Even this partial decoration seemed however to meet with approval, for the ten thousand hands commenced applauding vigorously, so much so that for a moment I fancied myself at the opera.

'Good heavens!' I thought, 'what a *claque* these hands would make!'

There was one thing, however, that puzzled me much as I reentered my room.

Why was it that Fair Rosamond could not lean out of the window? There was some mystery about it, I felt certain. I little thought in what manner or how soon that mystery was to be solved.

IX / ROSAMOND MAKES A GREEN BIRD

No sooner was my debt to the Hand thus satisfactorily acquitted, than, in the elation of the moment at having for the first time in my life paid a debt on the appointed day, I immediately applied my lips to the Ear on the inside, and communicated my desire for some pens, ink, and paper. In an incredibly short space of time, the Hands, doubtless stimulated by the magnificence of my reward, passed a quantity of writing materials up the stairs, and in a few moments I was at work on my three columns, being determined from that time not to fall into arrears for my board.

'It is of the utmost importance,' I thought, 'that I should be unfettered by pecuniary liabilities, if I would rescue Rosamond from the clutches of this vile Count. I feel convinced of being able to baffle all his enchantments. Yes, Hands, ye may close, Ears, ye may listen, Eyes, ye may watch, Mouths, ye may scream the alarm, but I will deceive ye all! There is no magician who can outconjure the imagination of man.'

Having mentally got rid of this fine sentence, I set myself regularly to work, and in a short space of time dashed off a stunning article on the hotel system of England as contrasted with that of America. If that paper was ever printed, it must have astonished the reader; for written as it was, under the influence of the enchantments of the Hotel de Coup d'Oeil, it mixed up the real and the ideal in so inextricable a manner, that it read somewhat like a fusion of alternate passages from Murray's guide-book and the *Arabian Nights'* Entertainments. Such as it was, however, it being finished, I folded it up and sent it by the Hand, with my compliments to Count Goloptious, begging that he should at the same time be informed that I was hungry, and wanted my breakfast. My message whirred along the ten thousand Mouths, and faded away down into the hall below.

I had scarcely re-entered my apartment when I heard the Blond Head open the window, and commence singing a strange wild sort of recitative, evidently with the view of attracting my attention. I listened, and found that it ran thus:–

Rosamond sings: 'I have a bird, a bird, who was born today.

'Today the sunshine entered him through his eyes; his glittering wings rustled in the breath of the warm noon, and he began to live.

'He is merry and bold and wise, and is versed in the mysteries that are sung by the Unseen Spirits.

'Yet he knows not the mystical joys of the silently growing forests.

'No egg ever contained him.

'No down, white and silken, ever sheltered him from the cold.

'No anxious, bright-eyed mother ever brought him the oily grain of the millet to eat, or sat on the neighboring tree-tops, singing the holy hymns of maternal love.

'He never heard the sonorous melodies of the trees, when the wind with rushing fingers strikes the various notes of the forest, and Ash and Oak, Alder and Pine, are blent in the symphonic chords of the storm.

'Ten white fingers made him.

'The great sun – too far away to know what it was doing – hatched him into life, and in the supreme moment when his little heart just commenced to beat, and his magical blood to ebb and flow through the mystic cells of his frame, his maker cast from her lips, through his gaping golden bill, a stream of song, and gifted him with voice.

'This is the bird, bold and merry and wise, who will shake my salvation from his wings.

'Ah! until the hour of my delivery arrives, he shall be fed daintily on preserved butterflies, and shall scrape his bill on a shell of pearl!'

I opened my window as the last words of this strange song died away, and I had scarcely done so when a bright green bird, with an orange bill and cinnamon-colored legs, flew from Rosamond's window into my room, and perched on the table. It was a charming bird. Its shape was somewhat like that of the mocking-bird – long, slender body, piquant head, and sweeping tail. Its color was of the most dazzling green, and its feathers shone like satin.

'Good morning, pretty bird,' said I, holding out my finger to my visitor, who immediately flew to my hand and established himself there.

'Good morning,' answered the Green Bird, in a voice so like Rosamond's that I was startled: 'I am come to breakfast with you.'

As the Green Bird spoke, a small bright feather dropped from its wing and fell slowly to the ground.

'I am delighted to have your society,' I replied, with the utmost courtesy, 'but I fear that I shall not be able to offer you any preserved butterflies. Nay, I have not as much as a beetle in pickle.'

'Don't mention it,' said the bird, with an off-hand flirt of his tail; 'I can put up with anything. Besides, you know, one can always fall back on eggs.'

To my surprise another bright green feather disengaged itself from the bird's plumage, and floated softly towards the carpet.

'Why, you'll lose all your feathers,' said I. 'Are you moulting?'

'No,' answered the bird, 'but I am gifted with speech on the condition that I shall lose a feather every time I use the faculty. When I lose all my feathers, which I calculate will not take place for about a year, I shall invent some artificial ornithological covering.'

'Gracious!' I exclaimed, 'what a figure – of speech you will be!'

At this moment the usual knock was heard at my door, on opening which I discovered a large tray covered with a snowy cloth, on which were placed a number of small porcelain covers, some bottles of red and white wine, a silver coffee-service, in short, everything necessary for a good breakfast.

X / BREAKFAST, ORNITHOLOGICALLY
CONSIDERED

In a few moments my repast was arranged on the table, at which I seated myself, the Green Bird perching on the edge of a pretty dish of scarlet fruits at which he pecked, occasionally moistening his golden bill in the slender glass of Barsac which I placed near him.

'Breakfast,' said the bird, looking at me with a glance of undisguised contempt while I was devouring a plate of *rognons au vin de champagne* – 'breakfast is a meal utterly misinterpreted by human beings. What can be more unhealthy or more savage than the English or American breakfast? The latter is a miracle of indigestibility. The elastic, hot cakes. The tough, over-cooked meats. The half-boiled, muddy coffee. The half-baked, alum-tempered bread. Breakfast should be a light meal, invigorating, yet not overloading – fruits to purify the palate and the physical system, and a little red wine to afford nourishment to the frame, and enable it to go through the work of the day. In the morning man arises refreshed, not exhausted; his frame needs but little support; it is only when the animal vitality has been used up by a hard day's labor, that the meal of succulent and carbonized food is required. The French make their breakfast too elaborate; the English too heavy; the Americans too indigestible.'

'Am I to understand, then,' I asked, 'that birds breakfast more sensibly than men?'

'Certainly,' replied the Green Bird. 'What is more delicate, and at the same time more easy of digestion, than the mucilaginous Caterpillar? The Dragon-fly, when carefully stripped of its corselet, is the lobster of the Insectivora. The green *acarus* is a dainty morsel, and the yellow roses sigh with relief when we gobble up their indolent enemy. The *coccinella*, or Lady-bird, is our turtle: with what dexterity is he stript of his upper shell and eaten palpitating!

'But the chief hygienic feature about the breakfast of us birds is, that we exercise in order that we may eat. Supposing the Blackbird, on withdrawing his head from under his crimson epaulet in the early morning, were merely to yawn, and stretch his wings, and, hopping lazily down branch by branch to the pool at the bottom of the tree on which he roosts, take his bath. That finished, we will suppose him retreating to his covert, when he rings a bell made of the blue campanula, and, being answered by an attendant Tom Tit, commands breakfast to be served. Tom Tit disappears, and after the usual absence returns with a meal of beetles, caterpillars, ripe cherries, and wild honey, neatly served on a satiny leaf of the Maple. Blackbird falls to and gorges himself. What an unhealthy bird he would be, compared with the Blackbird as he really is, stretching his wings at the first light of dawn, and setting off on a foraging expedition through the woods and fields! What glorious exercise and excitement there are in this chase after a breakfast! How all the physical powers are cultivated! The sight is sharpened. There is not a cranny in the bark of a tree, or a crevice in the earth, that the eye of the hungry bird does not penetrate. The extremist tip of the tail of a burrowing worm cannot remain undiscovered; he is whipped out and eaten in a moment. Then the long flight through the fresh air; the delicious draught of cool dew taken from time to time; the –'

'But,' said I, interrupting the Green Bird, who I began to perceive was an interminable talker, 'how is it possible for men to have the opportunity of pursuing their meals in the manner you describe? It would indeed present rather a ridiculous appearance, if at six o'clock in the morning I were to sally out, and run all over the fields turning up stones in order to find fried smelts, and diving into a rabbit burrow in the hope of discovering mutton chops *en papillotes*.'

'If I were a man,' said the Green Bird, sententiously, 'I would have my meals carefully concealed by the servants in various places, and then set to work to hunt them out. It would be twice as healthy as the present indolent method.'

Here he took another sip at the Barsac, and looked at me so queerly that I began to have a shrewd suspicion that he was drunk.

A brilliant idea here flashed across my mind. I would intoxicate the Green Bird, and worm out of him the reason why it was that the Blond Head was never able to stretch farther out of her window than the shoulders. The comicality of a drunken bird also made me favorable to the idea.

'As far as eating goes,' said I, 'I think that you are perhaps right; but as to drinking, you surely will not compare your insipid dew to a drink like this!' and, as I spoke, I poured out a glass of Richebourg, and handed it to the bird.

He dipped his bill gravely in it, and took one or two swallows.

'It is a fine wine,' he said sententiously, 'but it has a strong body. I prefer the Barsac. The red wine seems to glow with the fires of earth, but the white wine seems illumined by the sunlight of heaven.'

And the Green Bird returned to his Barsac.

XI / LEG-BAIL

'So the fair Rosamond made you,' I said carelessly.

'Yes, from terra-cotta,' answered the Green Bird; 'and, having been baked and colored, I came to life in the sun. I love this white wine, because the sun, who is my father, is in it'; and he took another deep draught.

'What induced her to construct you?' I asked.

'Why, with a view of escaping from this place, of course.'

'O, then you are to assist her to escape?'

'Not at all – you are to assist her. I will furnish her with the means.'

'What means?'

'With the wings.'

'The what?' I asked, somewhat astonished.

'The wings!'

'What the deuce does she want of wings? She is not going to escape by the window, is she?'

'Ha, ha, ha! Ho, ho, ho! He asks what Rosamond wants of wings!' And the bird, overcome with laughter at the ludicrousness of some esoteric jest, tumbled into his glass of Barsac, from which I rescued him draggled and dripping, all the more draggled as during our conversation he had been continually shedding his feathers.

'Well, what does she want of wings?' I asked, rather angrily, because a man does not like to see people laughing at a joke into the secret of which he is not admitted.

'To fly with,' replied the Green Bird, nearly choking with the involuntary draught of white wine he had swallowed during his immersion.

'But why does she want to fly?'

'Because she has no legs – that's the reason she wants to fly,' said the bird, a little crossly.

'No legs!' I repeated, appalled at this awful intelligence – 'no legs! O, nonsense! you must be joking.'

'No, I'm choking,' answered the Green Bird.

'Why, she is like Miss Biffin, then, born without legs. Heavens! what a pity that so lovely a head shouldn't have a leg to stand on!'

'She wasn't born without legs,' replied the Bird. 'Her legs are down stairs.'

'You don't mean to say that they have been amputated?'

'No. Count Goloptious was afraid she would escape; and as he wanted only her bust, that is, her brain, hands, and arms, he just took her legs away and put them in the storeroom. He'll take your legs away some day, too, you'll find. He wants nothing but heads in this hotel.'

'Never!' I exclaimed, horror-stricken at the idea. 'Sooner than part with my legs, I'd –'

'Take arms against him I suppose. Well, *nous verrons.*

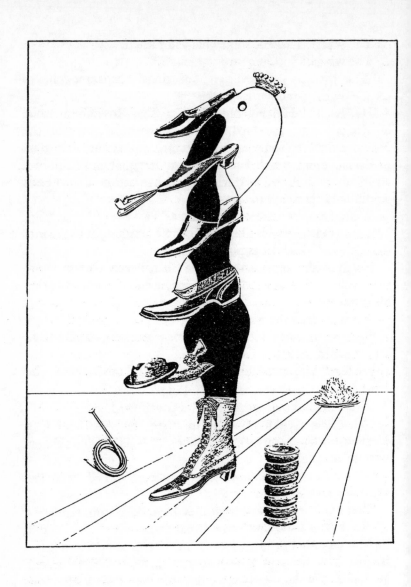

Gracious! what a lot of feathers I have shed!' suddenly continued the Bird, looking down at a whole pile of green feathers that lay on the floor. 'I'm talking too much. I shan't have a feather left soon if I go on at this rate. By the way, where is your mirror? I must reproduce myself.'

XII / HOLDING THE MIRROR UP TO NATURE

I handed the Green Bird a small dressing-glass which lay on the bureau – I mean, I placed it before him, for the impossibility of *handing* a bird anything will strike even the most uncultivated mind – and seated myself to, watch his proceedings with a considerable amount of curiosity.

I wish, before proceeding any further, to make a few random remarks on the looking-glass in America.

I take a certain natural pride in my personal appearance. It is of no consequence if my nose is a trifle too long, my chin too retreating, or my head too angular. I flatter myself that the elegance of a man's appearance does not depend on his individual traits, but upon his *tout ensemble*. I feel, when regarding myself in a well-constituted mirror, that, in spite of any trifling defects in detail, my figure on the whole is rather *distingué*.

In the matter of mirrors, I have suffered. The hotel and boarding-house keepers of this country – actuated doubtless by a wholesome desire to crush that pet fly called 'vanity,' with which the Devil angles for human souls – have, I am convinced, entered into a combination against the admiration of the human face divine by its owner.

Like Proteus, I find myself changing my shape wherever I go. At the Bunkum House, I am a fat boy. At the St. Bobolink, a living skeleton. Once I was seriously alarmed on inspecting myself for the first time in the glass – on an occasion when I had just taken possession of a new boarding-house – at discovering that one of my eyebrows was in the middle of my forehead. I had been informed by a medical student – since plucked – from whom I derived most of my chirurgical information, that paralysis not unfrequently produced such effects. I descended in some trepidation to the parlor, where I had an interesting interview with my landlady, who succeeded in removing the unpleasant impression from my mind that I was a victim to that unbecoming disease.

The glass was not, however, changed, and I never looked in it and beheld that eyebrow in the middle of my forehead, without the disagreeable sensation that in the end I should die a Cyclops.

The glass which I placed before the Green Bird possessed, I regret to say, certain defects in the plane of its surface, which rendered self-contemplation by its aid anything but an agreeable occupation. I know no man egotist enough to – as the novels say – 'spend hours before' such a mirror.

The Green Bird, as soon as he beheld himself in this abominable mirror, uttered a scream of disgust. I must say, that, on looking over his shoulder, the image formed by him in the glass was not a graceful one. He was humped, one leg was shorter than the other, and his neck looked as if it had just been wrung by a schoolboy.

What attracted my attention most, however, were certain peculiarities in the reflected image itself. It scarcely seemed a reflection. It was semi-substantial, and stood out from the surface of the glass in a sort of half-relief, that grew more and more positive every moment. In a few seconds more, the so-called image detached itself from the mirror, and hopped out on the table, a perfect counterpart of the Green Bird, only humped, with one leg shorter than the other, and a wry neck. It was an ornithological caricature.

The Green Bird itself now sidled away from its position before the mirror, and the Caricature Bird took his place. If the image cast by the former was distorted, no words can convey the deformity of the image cast by the latter. It was a feathered cripple. It was all hump. It stood on one long attenuated leg. Its neck was tortuous as the wall of Troy.

This rickety, ornithological image produced itself in the mirror, in precisely the same fashion as did its predecessor, and, after gradually growing into substance, detached itself from the polished surface, and came out upon the table, taking its position before the mirror, *vice* the first humpback resigned.

What the image cast by the third bird was like I cannot at all attempt to portray. It was a chaos of neck and humps and feathers. The reproduction, nevertheless, went on, and the prolific mirror kept sending forth a stream of green abortions, that after a little while were no longer recognizable as belonging to any species of animal in the earth below, or the heavens above, or the caverns that lie under the earth. They filled my room. Swarms of limping, wall-eyed, one-legged, green-feathered things hustled each other on the floor. My bed was alive with a plumed mass of deformity. They filled the air, making lame efforts at flight, and blindly falling to the floor, where they tumbled about in inextricable confusion. The whole atmosphere seemed thick with green feathers. A myriad of squinting eyes glittered before me. Quintillions of paralytic yellow bills crookedly gaped at me.

I felt myself treading on a thick carpet of soft, formless life. The fluttering of embryonic wings, the twittering of sickly voices, the ruffling of lusterless plumages, produced a continuous and vague sound that filled me with horror. I was knee-deep in the creatures. From out the distorting mirror they poured in a constant stream, like a procession of nightmares, and the tidemark of this sea of plumage rose higher and higher every instant. I felt as if I was about to be suffocated – as if I was drowning in an ocean of Green Birds. They were on my shoulders. Nestling in my hair. Crooning their loathsome notes into my ear. Filling my pockets, and brushing with their warm fuzzy breasts against my cheek. I grew wild with terror, and, making one desperate effort, struggled through the thick mass of life that pressed like a wall around me to the window, and, flinging it open, cried in a despairing voice: 'Rosamond! Rosamond! Save me, Rosamond!'

XIII / A STUPID CHAPTER, AND I KNOW IT

'What's the matter?' cried the Blond Head, appearing at her window, with all her curls in a flurry.

'Your Green Bird,' I answered, 'has been misconducting himself in the most abominable manner. He –'

'You surely have not let him get at a mirror?' screamed Rosamond.

'Unfortunately I have; and pretty things he has been doing with it. My room is full of Green Birds. If you don't call them away, or tell me how to get rid of them, I shall be killed, as the persons suspected of hydrophobia were formerly killed in Ireland, that is, I shall be smothered by a featherbed.'

'What a wretch of a bird to waste himself in such a foolish way, when he was so particularly wanted! But rest a moment. I will rid you of your unpleasant company.'

So saying, Rosamond withdrew her head from the window, and in a second or two afterwards a long shrill whistle came from her room, wild and penetrating as the highest notes of the oboe. The instant the Green Birds heard it, they all commenced jostling and crushing towards the open window, out of which they tumbled in a continual stream. As scarcely any of them could fly, only a few succeeded in reaching the sill of Rosamond's casement – the goal towards which they all struggled. The rest fell like a green cataract on the hard flags with which the yard underneath my window was paved. In this narrow enclosure they hustled, and crawled, and limped, and writhed, till the place, filled with such a mass of feathered decripitude, resembled an ornithological *Cour des Miracles*.

So soon as my room was cleared of the bird multitude, I commenced sweeping up the mass of green feathers which lay on the floor, and which had been shed by the original Green Bird, during his conversation with me at breakfast. While engaged in this task, I heard a laugh which seemed to come from my immediate neighborhood. I turned, and there sat the Green Bird on the mantelpiece, arranging what feathers he had left with his bill.

'What,' I said, 'are *you* there? Why, I thought you had gone with the rest of them!'

'Go with such *canaille* as that set!' answered the Green Bird, indignantly. 'Catch me at it! I don't associate with such creatures.'

'Then, may I ask, why the deuce did you produce all this *canaille* in my room, Green Bird?'

'It was your own fault. I intended to produce a few respectable and well-informed Green Birds, who would have been most entertaining society for you in your solitude, and materially aided you in your projects against Count Goloptious. But you presented me with a crooked mirror, and, instead of shapely and well-behaved Green Birds, I gave birth to a crowd of deformed and ill-mannered things, of no earthly use to themselves or anyone else. The worst of it is, they will build nests in the yard underneath, and bring forth a myriad of callow deformities, so that unless they are instantly destroyed you will have no peace from them.'

'I'll shoot them.'

'Where's your gun?'

'Well, then, I'll fish for them with a rod, line, and hook, as the Chinese fish for swallows, and then wring their necks.'

'Pooh! that won't do. They'll breed faster than you can catch them. However, you need not trouble yourself about them; when the time comes I'll rid you of them. I owe you something for having caused this trouble; beside, your Barsac was very good.'

'Will you take another glass?' I said.

'No, thank you,' politely replied the Green Bird. 'I have drunk enough already. About those feathers' (I had just swept the green feathers up into a little help) – 'what are you going to do with them?'

'To burn them, of course. I can't have them littering my room.'

'My dear sir,' said the Green Bird, 'those feathers are

immensely valuable. They will be needed to make Rosamond's wings. Put them into one of the drawers of the bureau, until they are wanted.'

I obeyed.

XIV / ON THE ADVANTAGES OF MARRYING A WITCH

'Now,' continued the bird, 'what are your plans for escape?'

'I haven't any, except a general idea of throttling Goloptious the next time he comes in here, gagging the Mouths, handcuffing the Hands, and bunging up all the Eyes, and then bolting somewhere or other with the Blond Head – that is, if we can recover her legs – say to Grace Church, where, with the blessing of Brown, we can become man and wife.'

'Are you not afraid to marry a sorceress?'

'Why should I be? Haven't I been continually calling every woman with whom I have been in love an enchantress; and writing lots of verses about the "spells" with which she encompassed me; and the magic of her glance, and the witchery of her smile? I'm not at all sorry, if the truth must be confessed, to meet an enchantress at last. She will afford me continual amusement. I need never go to see Professor Wyman, or Herr Dobler, or Robert Houdin. I can get up a little Parlor Magic whenever I choose. Fancy the pleasure of having Genii for servants, just like Aladdin! No Irish Biddies, to overroast your beef, and underboil your potatoes; to "fix" her mop of capillary brushwood with your private, particular hairbrush; to drink your brandy and then malign the cat; to go out on Sunday evenings, "to see his Reverence Father McCarthy," touching some matter connected with the confessional, and come home towards midnight drunk as an owl; to introduce at two in the morning, through the convenient postern of the basement, huge "cousins," whose size prevents you from ejecting them with the speed they merit, and who impudently finish their toddies before they obey your orders to quit. Genii have no cousins, I believe. Happy were the people in the days of Haroun Al Raschid.

'On these grounds I esteem it a privilege to marry a witch. If you want dinner, all you have got to do is to notify your wife. She does something or other, kills a black hen, or draws a circle in chalk, and lo! an attendant Genius, who lived four years in his last place, appears, and immediately produces an exquisite repast, obtained by some inscrutable means, known only to the Genii, and you dine, without having the slightest care as to marketing, or butcher's or baker's bills.

'Then again, if your wife knits you a purse, what more easy for her than to construct it after the pattern of Fortunatus's? If she embroiders you a pair of slippers, they can just as well as not be made on the last of the seven-league boots. Your smoking-cap can possess the power of conferring invisibility like that of Fortunio.

'You can have money when you want. You can dress better at church than any of her acquaintances, because all the treasures of Solomon are at her disposal, to say nothing of those belonging to Jamshid. You can travel faster than any locomotive. You can amuse yourself with inspecting the private lives of your friends. You can win at cards when you desire it. You can at any moment take up your drawing-room carpet, and make it sail away with you and all your earthly possessions to Minnesota, if you please. You can buy a block on Fifth Avenue, and build a palace in a night, and, in short, be always young, handsome, wealthy, happy, and respected. Marry an enchantress! why, it's even more profitable than marrying a Spirit Medium!'

'So you intend to marry Rosamond,' remarked the Green Bird, with the slightest sneer in the world.

'Certainly. Why not?'

'I don't see how you're to do it. She has not got any legs, and may not be able to get away from here. You won't have any legs in a day or two. You are both in the power of Count Goloptious;

and, even if you were to escape from your rooms, you would not be able to find the way out of the Hotel de Coup d'Oeil.'

'If I were forced to walk on my hands, I would bear Rosamond away from this cursed den of enchantment.'

'An excellent speech for Ravel to make,' replied the Green Bird, 'but I fancy that your education as an Acrobat has been neglected.'

'I think I see at what you are aiming,' I answered. 'You want to make terms. How much do you want to assist Rosamond and myself to escape? I learn from her song that you know the ropes.'

'I know the stairs and the doors,' said the Green Bird, indignantly, 'and that is more to the purpose.'

'Well, if you show us the way to get free, I will give you a golden cage.'

'Good.'

'You shall have as much hemp-seed as you can eat.'

'Excellent.'

'And as much Barsac as you can drink.'

'No,' here the Green Bird shook his head; 'I won't drink any more of your wine, but I want every morning a saffron cocktail.'

'A what?'

'A saffron cocktail. Saffron is our delight, not only of a shiny night, but also of a shiny morning, in all seasons of the year. It is the Congress Water of birds.'

'Well, you shall have a saffron cocktail.'

'And fresh groundsel every day.'

'Agreed.'

'Then I am yours. I will give my plot.'

THE GREEN BIRD MAKES A PLOT WHICH DIFFERS FROM ALL OTHER CONTEMPORARY PLOTS IN BEING SHORT AND SWEET.

'Sir,' said the Green Bird, 'you wish to escape.'

'Undoubtedly.'

'The chief enemies which you have at present to fear are the Hands that clutch, and the Mouths that betray.'

'I am aware of that fact.'

'It is necessary that you should visit Rosamond's room.'

'I would give my life to accomplish such a call.'

'All you want to enable you to accomplish it is a couple of lead-pencils and a paper of pins.'

'Well?'

'Well, that's my plot. Order them at the Ear, and when you get them I will show you how to use them'; and the Green Bird ruffled out his feathers and gave himself airs of mystery.

I immediately went to the Ear, and, removing the wax with which I had deafened it, ordered the articles as prescribed. I confess, however, that I was rather puzzled to know how with the aid of two lead-pencils and a paper of pins I was to baffle the spells of Goloptious.

XV / PREPARATIONS FOR FLIGHT

While awaiting the arrival of the desired articles, I heard Rosamond calling me through the window. I immediately obeyed the summons.

'An idea has just struck me,' said the Blond Head. 'I am exceedingly anxious, as you know, to get away from here, and I have no doubt with your aid might succeed in doing so, but how am I to take my trunks?'

'Your what?'

'Trunks. You did not suppose, surely, that I was staying here without a change of dress.'

'I always thought that imprisoned heroines contrived in some miraculous manner to get along without fresh linen. I have known, in the early days of my novel-reading, a young lady run through six volumes, in the course of which she was lost in forests, immersed in lakes, and imprisoned in dungeons, in a single white skirt and nothing on her head. I often thought what a color that white skirt must have been at the end of the novel.'

'O,' said Rosamond, 'I have quite a wardrobe here.'

'Well, I'm afraid you'll have to leave it behind.'

'What! leave all those ducks of dresses behind! Why, I'd rather stay here forever than part with them. It's so like a man to say, in the coolest manner in the world, "Leave them behind." ' And the Blond Head here agitated her curls with a certain tremulous motion, indicative of some indignation.

'My dear, you need not be angry,' I said soothingly. 'Perhaps, after all, we can manage to get your trunks away also. How much luggage have you got?'

'I will read you the list I made of it,' answered Rosamond.

This is her list – I jotted it down at the time in pencil. The remarks are my own:–

One large trunk, banded with iron, and containing my evening dresses.

One large square trunk containing my bonnets, two dozen. (The excusable vanity of an individual having nothing but a head.)

One cedar chest containing my furs. (At this point I ventured a joke about a cedar chest being a great deal too good for such minkses. I was promptly suppressed by the dignified statement that they were sables.)

One circular box for carrying the incompressible skirt. (Doubtless an expansive package.)

A bird-cage.

A case for artificial flowers.

A feather case. (Containing the last feather which is supposed to be fatal to the Camel.)

A willow basket for bonnets. (More bonnets!)

Three large trunks. (Contents not stated – suspicious circumstance.)

Four small trunks. (What male who has ever travelled with a lady does not remember with terror her *small* parcels? The big ones gravitate naturally to the baggage-car; but you are requested to see after the little ones yourself. You carry them in your arms, tenderly, as if they were so many babies. What lamentations if they slip – and they are always doing it – and fall in the street! Something very precious must be inside. In the cars, you have to stow them away under the seat so that you have no room for your legs. Woe to you if one is lost or mislaid. It always contains *the* very thing of all others which the owner would not have lost for worlds.)

A bandbox. (The bandbox is the most terrible apparatus connected with the locomotion of females. It refuses utterly to accommodate itself to travel. Its lid comes off. It will fit into no shaped vehicle. Of its own accord it seems to place itself in positions favorable to its being sat upon. When crushed or in any way injured, it is capable of greater shabbiness of appearance than any other article of luggage.)

A dressing-case.

A portable bath.

An easel. (Easily carried.)

Three boxes of books. (A porter who was once removing my luggage called my attention to the weight of the box in which I had packed my books. They were certainly very heavy, and yet I had selected them with the greatest care.)

Here Rosamond stopped, and then proposed going over the list again, as she was sure she had forgotten something.

I respectfully declined the repetition, but asked her by what possible means she expected to transport such a quantity of luggage out of the Hotel de Coup d'Oeil.

'You and the Green Bird can manage it, I suppose,' she answered; 'and I wish you would make haste, for I am getting very weary of not being able to walk. I shall so enjoy having my legs back again.'

'Have you any idea where Count Goloptious put them?'

'O yes. They are in some cellar or other in a bin, with a number of other legs.'

'Are the bins numbered?'

'Certainly.'

'Do you know the number of your bin?'

'No. How should I?'

'It strikes me as rather awkward that you do not. For supposing that the Green Bird and myself succeed in getting down stairs in search of your legs, if we don't know the number of the bin we shall have some difficulty in finding the right ones, and it would be very disagreeable if you had to walk off with another person's legs.'

'I never thought of that,' said Rosamond, gravely. 'A misfit would be horribly uncomfortable.'

XVI / A THRILLING CHAPTER

We were certainly in a very unpleasant fix. To go down stairs on a wild-goose chase among the bins in search of the legs of the Blond Head would be anything but agreeable.

'Can you not make any pair do for the present?' I asked.

'Any pair? Certainly not. Could you get along with any other head but your own?'

The question rather took me aback. I confessed that such a change was not at all to be desired.

'Then go,' said the Blond Head, 'and search for them.'

'Faint heart,' etc.; a musty adage came into my head, and I answered, 'I will do so.' Turning to the Green Bird, I asked, 'Will you come to the cellars?'

'Yes, at once,' was the answer.

'Lead the way, then; you must be better acquainted here than I am.'

The Green Bird led the way down the stairs, with all the

hands before us; but not one moved now. Down! down! at least an hundred flights, then through a hall, and into a vast chamber black as midnight.

'How are we to find the legs in this plutonian darkness?' I asked.

'Silence!' said the Green Bird, and a falling feather aroused an echo that sounded like the beating of an hundred drums; 'speak not if you would succeed!'

In silence I followed on through the cavernous chamber with its pitchy walls – on, still on. At last a small blue light appeared burning in the distance like the eye of a tiger. As we approached, it gradually increased in size, until, at last, as we neared it, it became magnified into an opening some sixty feet wide. Beyond, burned a lake of deadly blue sulphur, shedding a pale unearthly light. As we passed through the opening, a figure suddenly appeared before us. It was that of an old man. He carried a stick in his right hand, and walked with a feeble gait, but, what struck me as rather peculiar, his head, instead of being on his shoulders, he carried under his left arm.

'Who are you?' he asked, speaking from the head under his arm.

'I am an author,' I replied.

'Look there?' he said, as he pointed to the burning lake.

I looked, and beheld what I had not before noticed. It was inhabited. Hundreds of poor wretches were there, burning and writhing in the seething flame.

'Who are those wretched beings?' I queried, in terror.

'Ha! ha! ha!' laughed the old man. 'Those are authors!'

'Why doomed to a residence here?'

'Because, when on the earth beyond, they failed to fulfil their mission. They lost sight of their goal. They digressed from the path of honor. They –'

'I see. They went it blind.'

'Exactly.'

'There,' and he pointed to a floating head near the edge of

the lake – 'there is a plagiarist. His is the A No. 1 degree. There,' and he pointed to another, 'is one who published and edited a newspaper.'

'His offense?' I asked.

'Blackmailing. There is one who wrote flash novels.'

'Jack Sheppard. *The Bhoys,*' I muttered.

'Ay; you be wise; avoid the broad path; keep faith; be true. And now what seek you here?'

I told him my errand.

'And you hope to find the legs?'

'I do.'

'Come, then, with me. Here, carry my head.'

I took the head, and, with the Green Bird by my side, followed the singular old man. He led us round by the lake, so close that, at times, the heat seemed to scorch my clothing. Presently he stopped opposite a great door of blue veined marble. Pushing that open, we entered a large and brilliantly lighted apartment. Here, upon every side, countless legs protruded from the wall. As we entered, the legs all at once commenced kicking as though they would eject us from their abode.

The old man took his head from us, and, putting it under his arm, commanded the legs to desist from their threatening attitudes. In an instant they all fell dormant.

'Here,' he said, 'are the legs of all who have ever slept in the Hotel de Coup d'Oeil, and here you will find those of the Blond Head.'

'But how am I to know them?' I said.

'That I cannot tell you.'

'I can tell them,' said the Green Bird, now speaking for the first time since we left the darkness; and it flew around the room, stopping to look at now one pair of legs, now another. At last it stopped opposite a remarkably crooked pair of limbs. 'Here they are,' he said.

'Nonsense! it cannot be. Such a beauty as the Blond Head never propelled on such pedals as those.'

'It is true,' answered the bird. 'Take them down, and see.' I seized the legs, and with a sudden jerk pulled them from their place. What was my surprise on finding Count Goloptious before me. The legs were his.

'Ha!' he exclaimed, 'you would trick me, but I have watched you. The Blond Head is safe.'

'Safe!' I echoed.

'Ay, safe, safe in my stronghold, the Hotel de Coup d'Oeil.'

''Tis false!' cried the Green Bird. 'She is here!' As it spoke, it flew to a small door in the wall which I had not before noticed. Tapping with its beak against it, it opened instantly, and, looking in, I beheld the Blond Head complete. Never did I behold a being so beautiful as she seemed to me at that glance. Grace, beauty, voluptuousness – well, imagine all the extensive descriptions of female loveliness you have ever read in two-shilling novels, put them all altogether, and pile on as much more, and then you have her description.

'Fair Rosamond,' I exclaimed, as I started forward to gain her – 'Fair Rosamond, you shall be saved.'

'Never!' cried Count Goloptious – 'never! Beware, rash youth! You have dared to criticize Italian opera, you have dared write political leaders, you have dared theatrical managers, you have dared a fickle public – all this you have done, but brave not me. If you would be safe, if you value your life, go, depart in peace!'

As he spoke, I felt the chivalric blood fast coursing through my veins. Go, and leave the fair being I loved in the power of a monster? No, I resolved upon the instant that I would die with her, or I would have her free.

'Count,' I exclaimed in passionate tones, 'I defy thee. I will never forsake yon wretched lady.'

'Then your doom is sealed.' He stamped three times upon the floor, and instantly the Green Bird disappeared. The place was wrapped in darkness. I felt myself borne through the murky, foul air of the cavern through which we had first passed, with the rapidity of a cannon-ball. Emerging from it, I found myself in the arms of the Count; by his side stood the old man with his head under his arm.

'Here,' cried the Count, 'is the nine hundred and twentieth. Eighty more, and we are free.'

A demoniacal laugh burst from the old man as he took me, unable to resist him, from Goloptious. 'Go, go to your brother authors, to the blue lake of oblivion. Go,' he exclaimed with a sardonic bitterness, as he pitched me from him into the burning lake.

A wild shriek. The burning sulphur entered my ears, my eyes, my mouth. My senses were going, when suddenly a great body, moving near, struck me. The liquid opened, and closed over me. I found myself going down, down. At last, I struck the bottom. One long scream of agony, and –

XVII / HOW IT ALL HAPPENED

'Good gracious! is that you? Why, how came you there?'
    'Dunno.'
    'Bless me, you've almost frozen. Come, up with you.'
    'What! Bunkler, that you? Where's the Blond Head?'
    'Blond what? You've been drinking.'
    'Where's Count Goloptious?'
    'Count the deuce; you're crazy.'
    'Where's the Green Bird?'
    'You're a Green Bird, or you wouldn't lie there in the snow. Come, get up.'
    In an instant I was awake. I saw it all. 'What's the time?' I asked.
    'Just two!'
    Could all that have happened in an hour! Yes. The Hotel de Coup d'Oeil. The Blond Head. The Green Bird. The Count. The Blue Lake. The Hands. The Legs. The Eyes, the everything singular, were the creations of Pilgarlik's

Burgundy. I had slipped in the snow at the door, and was dreaming.

The cold had revived me, and I was now shivering. I arose. My friend and fellow-boarder, Dick Bunkler, who had been tripping it on the light fantastic toe at a ball in the Apollo, was before me; and lucky it was for me that he had gone to that ball, for had I lain there all night, the probability is Coroner Connery would have made a V off my body, next day.

'How came you to lie there *outside* the door?' asked Dick.

'The door is fast; my night-key wouldn't work.'

'Night-key! ha! ha! night-key!'

I looked at my hand, and beheld what? My silver pencil-case, – the only piece of jewelry I ever possessed.

Dick opened the door, and in a very short time was engaged in manufacturing the 'Nightcap' which I had promised myself an hour before. Over it I told my dream in the snow, and we enjoyed a hearty laugh at the effect of the bottle of Burgundy which passed from HAND TO MOUTH.

THE COUNCIL OF LOVE

Oscar Panizza

In Heaven. An intimate council room in blue. A substitute throne, comfortable and plain. God the Father, Mary, Christ, the Devil. The first three are seated. The Devil stands before them, leaning on one foot and supporting the other with his hands. He wears a black close-fitting costume, is very slender, close-shaven with a fine-cut face, but his features wear an expression that is decadent, worn, embittered. He has yellowish complexion. His manners recall those of a Jew of high breeding. He leans on one foot; the other is drawn up. He stands erect.

GOD THE FATHER (*serious and to the point*):
My friend, the reason We sent for you . . . a very special
mission is involved . . . (*He hesitates*) . . . which calls for
a certain dexterity. . . . I am aware of your intellectual
gifts . . .

(*The Devil bows.*)

. . . and I just wonder . . . (*He hesitates*) . . . What is
involved is, uh . . . a being, uh . . . a thing, which . . .
uh, an influence, which might just conceivably be able
to restore to the path of virtue . . . uh, and to true
decency . . . that disgusting and abandoned humanity
that craves . . .

(*The Devil makes a courtly gesture of sympathy and inner understanding.*)

. . . What I'm thinking of is some sort of punishment they will really feel . . . uh, so that . . . uh . . . (*turning to Christ*) My dear Son, You tell him. Words don't come easily to Me. I've always been one to act. I've never put much stock in words.

CHRIST (*rising with difficulty, thinking for a moment, then speaking easily*):
Sir! . . . It occurred to Us to turn to you for help . . . in a matter . . . which may prove to be to our mutual advantage. . . . I do not mean to imply – and I say this explicitly at the outset in order to avoid any possible misunderstanding – that you would in any way relinquish your claim over mankind in the earthly sphere.

(*The Devil makes a gesture of understanding and protest, as if to say that the thought had never occurred to him.*)

On the contrary, you would have even more complete control over this sphere than before. What is involved is a compromise, an agreement, a readjustment of the boundaries of our previously defined, reciprocal powers, without any loss of authority for either of the contracting parties, whereby your unimpeachable skill, your acuity, your tact, your indulgent cooperativeness, your culture, your . . . your . . .

He begins to cough, breathes with difficulty, moans and pants. His throat rattles. His eyes bulge. His brow is covered with sweat. He is going into an asthma attack.

MARY (*springing forward while the Devil feigns with great elegance a discreet embarrassment*):
Take it easy, Son. You shouldn't try to talk. It only makes You worse. After all, You're sick. (*Turning to the Devil with complicity*) My dear friend, We need your help – and it won't be at all necessary for anyone to know that you had anything to do with it.

(*The Devil protests reassuringly.*)

Come on, give us a hand. You won't regret it. (*She winks at him.*) You know what I mean.

(*She points to God, meaning that He's deaf, old, and feeble and cannot be an obstacle. The Devil bows.*)

Now, in plain language, here's the situation. Someone (*she points to the Old Man*) took it into his head, most regrettably I must say, to show Us a little scene that occurred in the Pope's Palace in Rome . . . in his rooms. What's that Pope's name, anyway?

THE DEVIL (*very cooperative*):
Ah, Alexander the Sixth, Rodrigo Borgia.

MARY:
That's it, Borgia. . . . Oh, and what a scandal it was. Ghastly! And at Easter Communion!

GOD THE FATHER (*suddenly bursting into unrestrained vulgarity*):
Ugh! Devil's filth! Ugh! Devil's filth! Ugh! Devil's filth!

CHRIST (*stirring from his lethargy and agreeing in a dull voice*):
Yes, Devil's filth! Ugh! Devil's filth!

THE DEVIL (*in great confusion, annoyed, disturbed*):
> You will forgive me . . . under the circumstances . . . I
> must decline . . . it becomes impossible . . .

> (*He takes a step backward and is about to withdraw.*)

GOD THE FATHER (*turning to the Devil in a conciliatory tone*):
> For God's sake, no! I didn't mean you . . .

THE DEVIL (*offended*):
> It was my impression . . .

GOD THE FATHER:
> No, no! . . . A thousand times no! It's not true! It just
> slipped out . . . an old habit . . . I forgot . . .

THE DEVIL (*returning, elegant, conciliatory, with a bitter smile,
flicking a bit of dust from a sleeve*):
> Please . . . please . . .

MARY:
> No, no, my friend, you're one of Us. There can be no
> question about that. And no question of differences.
> We need you far too much. (*Directing her words loudly
> and pointedly to the Old Man*) We shall never allow Our
> dearest cousin, Our ally, Our dearly beloved brother
> . . . to be insulted.

> (*The Devil bows courteously.*)

> Now, to make a long story short, here's where we stand:
> It has been contemplated in high places (*pointing to
> God*) that it would be just as well to destroy the
> entire human race. This idea, however, has now been
> abandoned because of more important considerations,
> and we now prefer a more conventional type of revenge.

Something old-fashioned . . . along the lines of the Flood or Original Sin. That's why we consequently need someone, something, an influence, a force, a person, a disease, some little thing that will put a stop to the lewdness of humanity, especially of the Neapolitans and Romans . . . from a sexual point of view. Oh! You know what I mean! (*She pours a little cologne onto her handkerchief and holds it to her nose, breathes in slightly, while making eyes at the Devil over the handkerchief.*) Something that will call a halt to the bestiality of all those males and females who seem to be quite unaware that contact and penetration are purely incidental and to be tolerated only within the absolute limits of the needs of reproduction. Oh, it's unbearable! (*Breathes in more cologne.*) Surely you see what I mean!

THE DEVIL (*in a deep bass, somewhat stagy*):
I see what You mean.

GOD THE FATHER (*roaring*):
Yes, yes! Put a stop to it!

CHRIST (*with the voice of a consumptive*):
Yes, yes! Put a stop to it!

THE DEVIL (*after reflection*):
I presume it should be something quite painful?

MARY (*extending her lace handkerchief toward the Devil and nodding vigorously; speaking as if for the two others as well as for herself*):
Exactly. It should be very painful.

GOD THE FATHER (*looking on glassily, seeming not to understand, groaning finally in agreement in a thick, rasping voice*):

Yes, yes!

CHRIST (*still in attack, recovering slowly, breathing heavily*):
Yes, yes!

THE DEVIL (*standing with head bowed in thought, two fingers against his lips*):
Should this thing follow as an immediate consequence?

MARY:
Of course! Of course it should!

GOD THE FATHER (*still staring glassily*):
Of course! Of course!

Christ tries to repeat, 'Of course! Of course!' but is too slow and breaks into Mary's following speech. Mary pays no attention and continues, waving her handkerchief to silence her Son. The latter follows her every movement with greedy eyes.

MARY (*to the Devil*):
You're on the right track, my friend. Oh, I can see that We're going to be very pleased.

The Devil gives Mary a short, sharp glance, then sinks again into his thoughts. After a long pause, during which only the throat-rattle of Christ is audible, he speaks.

THE DEVIL (*emphasizing and accenting his words in a way of his own*):
Well, then, we'll have to put the sting, the disease, uh, the something . . . (*raising his finger as if taking aim*) . . . into the thing itself . . . into the . . . hm! (*clearing his throat as if to make a point*) . . . into the contact!

MARY (*very worldly*):
Lovely! Perfectly lovely!

GOD THE FATHER (*not understanding, looks on with staring, bulging eyes. He reproduces the intonation rather than the sense of Mary's words*):
Yes, yes, yes.

Christ also tries to imitate, but can't get the words out. He becomes alarmed at his own predicament, stares first at God the Father, then at Mary. He finally produces a rhythmical, inarticulate 'Ah! Ah! Ah!'

THE DEVIL (*after observing Christ's effort with a cool stare, yet without interrupting his own thoughts, continues with emphasis*):
We should introduce the infection into the secretion at the moment of sexual union.

MARY:
Oh? What do you mean? Oh, but that is very interesting! (*Sits up straight on her chair.*)

God the Father and Christ, who seem to have understood this time, sit staring goggle-eyed at the Devil.

DEVIL (*repeating the thought he has just had, as if to fix it in his own mind*):
We should introduce the infection into the secretion at the moment of sexual union.

MARY:
You mean the seed? (*She holds her handkerchief for a moment before her mouth as if she were trying to swallow something unpleasant.*)

THE DEVIL (*interrupting*):

No, no! Not the seed! Not the egg! Otherwise the children would be affected, and once they've been corrupted and made aware, we'll have had it! No, they must not be allowed to escape! We must leave the seed and egg alone so that human procreation can go merrily on. What we must find is some small by-product that will infect the aggressor as he plunges ahead, driven by instinct; something that will appear simultaneously with seed and egg and, as with snakes, is equally harmful to both parties, both partners in the game of sex – forgive me if my words offend –

(*Mary raises her eyebrows to indicate that she has understood.*)

so that the man can infect the woman or the woman the man, or, more ideally, both can infect each other, thoroughly unaware, completely caught up in their frenzy, in the fraud of total happiness.

(*He makes a gesture with his hand, as if to ask Mary if she has understood. Mary responds with delight, waving her handkerchief to say that she had indeed understood.*)

Babbling like babies, they'll rush blindfolded into the whole hideous mess!!!

MARY:

It's glorious! It's charming! It's diabolical! But how will you ever do it?

God the Father and Christ continue to stare goggle-eyed.

THE DEVIL:

Ah, Madam, that will be my problem.

MARY:

Very well, but only under one condition. Whatever you do, mankind must continue to have need of redemption.

THE DEVIL (*with great self-control*):

Mankind will always remain in need of redemption.

MARY:

And mankind must always remain capable of redemption.

THE DEVIL (*raising his arms, like a salesman, to shoulder height*):

Capable of redemption! After I've polluted them! And to order yet! That's asking a lot!

MARY (*springing down from her throne and retreating hastily in the direction of God the Father and Christ*):

In that case it's all off! If We can't redeem mankind any more, then what's the point?

(*God the Father and Christ raise their hands in despair. Christ, who is somewhat better, begins now to follow with more lively interest.*
The Devil turns on his right heel, smiles sardonically, and shrugs his shoulders. He feigns regret. Very much the Jewish merchant. A painful moment. The deal seems to be off. Pause.)

MARY (*returning slowly to her throne in order to divert their attention, suddenly asking the Devil in a friendly voice*):

By the way, how's your foot?

THE DEVIL (*playing her game*):

Oh, so-so! No better! But no worse, actually! Oh, god!

(*Hitting his shorter leg a blow.*) There's no change any more! Blasted thing!

MARY (*in a lower voice*):
Your fall did that?

(*The Devil, not reacting, is silent for a while; then he nods gravely.*)

(*Very cordially*) Well, anyway, how's Grandma?

THE DEVIL (*equally cordially*):
Lilith? Oh, thank You, very well!

MARY:
And the little ones?

THE DEVIL:
Thank You, thank You! They're fine.

Another pause. Mary, undecided, goes finally over to God the Father, with whom she speaks for a moment in a low voice. Thereupon . . .

GOD THE FATHER (*obviously having received instructions*):
Come now, my friend, you should be able to think up something that will hurt humanity without destroying it completely! Then, afterwards, We'll redeem it again! Won't We, My Son?

CHRIST:
We'll redeem humanity again!

MARY:
We've got to redeem humanity again!

THE DEVIL:
> The assignment is too difficult! I'm supposed to find something that is disgusting, amusing, and lethal at the same time! Then I'm supposed to get at them directly, violently, in their secret, amorous relationships and poison them right there on the spot! If those are the conditions, then the soul has got to be a part of the deal! That's where the soul is!

GOD THE FATHER (*surprised*):
> That's where the soul is?

CHRIST (*also surprised, but repeating mechanically*):
> That's where the soul is?

MARY (*affirmatively, half to herself, as if she were remembering*):
> That's where the soul is. . . .

THE DEVIL (*to God, after a pause, rather sarcastically*):
> My God, You're the Creator, aren't You? You ought to know!

GOD THE FATHER (*reluctantly*):
> We . . . uh . . . no longer create. We are tired. Besides, the area of earth and sense lies in your sphere. So make up your mind! Defile the soul if you must, but it must remain redeemable.

CHRIST (*still weak, attempting to repeat after God, but getting only as far as*):
> Defile . . . the . . . soul . . .

THE DEVIL (*to God the Father*):
> It should make them want to make love, You say, but at the same time act as a poison?

GOD THE FATHER:
Naturally, otherwise you won't catch them!

CHRIST (*breathing again*):
Passion . . . makes . . . them . . . blind.

MARY:
Well, if you want to catch mice, don't use pepper.

GOD THE FATHER:
Stick your nose into your witches' kettles! You'll find plenty of stuff! That Hell of yours is well supplied with everything! You're a good cook when it comes to stews like that! Stir it up! Mix it up! Create! Whip up something!

MARY:
At all events, it should be something very seductive. If possible, something feminine.

CHRIST:
Yes, something very seductive.

THE DEVIL (*following a train of thought*):
Libidinous and destructive at the same time? And still not ultimately destructive to the soul?

ALL THREE (*at the same time and all together*):
Libidinous! Destructive! Seductive! Lethal! Lustful! Horrible! Something to set the brain and blood on fire!

GOD THE FATHER:
But not the Soul! Because of contrition! Because of despair!

THE DEVIL (*suddenly terminating his train of thought*):
Stop! I've got something! I must have a word with Herodias! (*Half to himself*) Libidinous and destructive at the same time! (*Out loud*) I want to show you something!

MARY:
The Lord be praised!

THE DEVIL (*turning to leave*):
I think I've got it!

GOD THE FATHER:
Bravo! Bravo!

MARY:
Bravo! Bravo!

CHRIST:
Bravo! Bravo!

ALL THREE (*delighted, rising as far as they are able*):
Bravo, good Devil, bravo! Bravissimo!

THE DEVIL (*bidding them farewell and snapping his fingers as he leaves*):
I'll be right back!

The Devil leaves. As he opens the door, he sees several younger angels outside who have been eavesdropping. He catches the nearest one by the wings and roughs him up. The angel runs off with the others amid frightful screams. One then sees the Devil open a trapdoor through which he descends, closing it after him. The three Divinities disappear into the right wings as the scene changes.

THE WEIRD JOURNEY

Mervyn Peake

ONCE UPON A time-theory, when alone on the great bed, I found that no sooner had my head left the pillow than I fell wide awake. How far I fell I cannot say, but the light was brilliant about me and the shrill cries of birds were loud in my ears – so loud they seemed, that I could not tell whether they were in my brain or whether, all around my head and limbs, they spiralled in a flight too fleet for vision.

I could remember nothing save that I had come out of darkness – a kindly, muffling darkness, a daylight darkness, a summer of sepia, and that I was now in brilliance, the brilliance of night, very thrilling to the bones, where everything seemed diamond clear and *close*, frighteningly close, and palpable, stereoscopic, and edged, and a kind of dye-like lucency coloured the merest grain of rock – the smallest frond.

I could not tell what size I was at first, but a sensation of height pervaded me, and glancing downwards it was not easy at first-sight to perceive what footwear I favoured, although not a cloud lay between my head and a brand new pair of snakeskin striding boots. Not only were they of the stoutest and most brilliant snakeskin, but the speed at which they crossed one another startled me, for it was obvious that they were bound upon some journey with a purpose most immediate. I had no more idea of where they were going than I had of why my hands were raised and my fingertips joined and directed forwards at the level of my heart like a prow of a ship. But I knew well enough that to try and stay my progress would be futile, for I was on my way. Where? I did not know. Nor did I, at this juncture care. Enough, it seemed to me, that I was on my way, after years of stillness.

I lifted my eyes from the deft and purposeful progress

of my snakeskin covered feet and turned my attention to my other garments, which were, wherever possible, swept out in stiff horizontal flight, the two tails of my tie for instance, parting at the knot, flew over either shoulder like pennants, and my jacket, black and tarnished though it was, spread like the wings of some great fowl behind me – some fowl of hell, the state of whose matted nest (no doubt within the whorled throat of some blood-patched pinnacle) I shuddered to dwell upon. But what did it matter – sinister as was my flying jacket, it could not harm me, and I never so much as glanced over my shoulder a second time but turned my eyes to what lay ahead and about me.

I had no sensation of speed, though objects sped by me, less swiftly upon my right-hand than upon my left, it is true, but very swiftly indeed for all that – and most speedily of all above my head where parrots tore past with bibles in their beaks.

One after another they flooded past, red, orange, yellow, green, blue, indigo, violet, in that order of rotation, the leaves of Genesis fluttering in the beak of the scarlet bird, Leviticus in the next and so on to Joshua, after which the wild story of Eden would again rattle its green pages in my ear as it sped by, and I closed my eyes for a few moments while my feet paced on. After a while I was able to open my eyes and take no notice at all of the spectrum birds, save when occasionally all the parrots would open their murderous beaks and cry 'Amen', shutting their mouths again with a clang before the bibles could overbalance and fall fluttering. But even this I grew used to and I was able to concentrate on what lay further afield.

On my right-hand a green ocean, somewhat the colour of an unripe apple, coughed and sneezed. The sands along its margin were covered with innumerable deckchairs, the canvas of each dyed in uniform stripes of red and white. Very neat they were, very clean – in groups, or aloof as they favoured. But no one sat in them, nor was anyone to be seen on that wide, clear strand.

As far as eye could see little circles of foam slid about the feet of the most seaward chairs.

On my left, a grey mountain-range was dotted with prawn-coloured villas, each one a replica of its neighbour. In the garden of every villa sat something that was smoking a pipe. I turned my head away quickly.

Ahead of me was the road that I travelled. It was cold and deathly white with artificial snow, and it was then that I noticed a most peculiar thing. Observing that in the distance the white road was speckled down its centre, I dropped my eyes gradually until, as my vision approached my own feet, I realized that I was looking at footprints. They rushed to meet me, or so it seemed, down the long strip of artificial snow, and as I was propelled forward and over them I found that my feet fell unerringly into their shallow, fish-shaped basins. Try as I would, I could not evade them. Footstep after footstep fell as though pre-ordained into its place. I tried to leap sideways, but a kind of magnetism drew the swift soles of my snakeskin boots into the flying footprints. But this was not all. Peering at each in turn, immediately before the descent of my either foot into its basin, I could see that the footprints were *mine*, the little snakeskin scales showing their imprints in the pressed snow. There was no doubt of it – let alone the simpler proof that my feet, long, slender and pigeon-toed, had no duplicates – nor indeed any rivals among the feet of the world.

I could not escape the answer. I trod upon myself, upon my past; my early days; upon my childhood when I journeyed down white roads of wonder and innocence that were like the echoes of things long known and temporarily forgotten. But that was all very well. My childhood had not been like that. It had been surrounded by high grey acres of wall-paper and photographs gone yellow of marriage groups and dogs' heads and faded cricket teams. And huge aunts sat bolt upright in the corners of half-lit rooms and filled them up, and uncles stumbled across halls with guns under their arms, trailing their gammy legs. And I had been a wicked child. There had been no snow-white wonder or innocence about me. On the contrary I had made everyone irritated – and there was nothing strange, that I could remember, to account for this experience. Everything had been so very ordinary – with the great walnut tree outside the nursery window, with the white broken branch caught and kept from falling among the green leaves. And I was greedy – and my parents were weak and everything was very dreary. What had all this got to do with these footprints I trod in – these relics of myself? I could find no answer.

I began to be irritated by the way in which my body was propelling itself forward in complete disregard to any objective. It is absurd enough to find yourself on your way somewhere or another without wishing to reach any such place, but to travel like an automaton to an *unknown* destination appeared to me to be unhealthy and ludicrous. I had lost all interest in the fact that it was strange for it was no longer so, but hideously dreary.

My legs evidently had more moral power and vision than I had myself and for a moment I flamed into a sudden temper and would have stamped the very feet that bore me had I been able to control them. I began to hate them. That there were two of them angered me. The mere fact that the very principle of perambulation necessitated a couple of feet held little weight with me. Two feet were twice as annoying as one when they travelled of their own volition and had me in their power and propelled me onwards in a nameless land. And then I began to be frightened – a nameless land. It was the words which frightened me more than the circumstance – and I began to shake as I walked and my mind began to be horrified at the possibilities which this progress opened up.

Suppose that I were taken to the verge of some precipice and were compelled to walk out into space . . . Suppose that they took me to some sharp den of fangs – or to some midnight cellar full of splashing water where the backs of soft beasts rose intermittently above the cold surface, and occasionally some wet and yellow head that mewed and sank again . . .

Or suppose that my feet took me to some vast hall full of desks and carried me to the only empty one – hacked and scored by decades of penknife wounds, mutilated by the initials of whipped boys who could not understand their algebra . . . who wept and suffered from the horror and the whirling of algebraic symbols . . . who were ill because of algebra, and died of it; while at the end of the great hall the master, whose face had no features, turned his blank mask at me, so that my wrists and forehead sweated with fear and my inky hand could not hold the slippery pen, and the algebra danced about the paper like flies on a window-pane . . .

Or supposing my feet took me into a land of whiteness where no colours could breathe, and that I screamed for colour but none came; only whiteness like a theory, draining the love from life.

I struck my head to kill the fear that now possessed me, and in an effort to distract my mind I looked to left and right. But the deckchairs were still standing in their thousands by the sea. The long endless sands curved over into the horizon. The foam still circled the legs of the most seaward chairs – there were no seagulls, but the sea was still bright and the coughing and sneezing from its million little waves sounded thinly and very far away – very forlorn – and terrible – for where were the spades, the sand castles, and the bathing huts and donkeys, the aunts and ugly women, the kites and the children? Oh far away – far away, in some holiday from school – when, if heartache were mine, I could no longer recall it.

And on my left the range of grey mountains and the pink villas, but I turned my head away quickly, for fear of seeing the things in the gardens with pipes in their mouths. I longed for death, I ached and prayed for all volition to cease – for the unutterable consummation of final atrophy.

And yet, how weird it was, I felt no fatigue. My snakeskin boots flew on beneath me, and my body was light as a breath of air. And then it was that having turned my head away for some time from the landscape on my left, and the seascape on my right, a sense of uneasiness over and above my agony caused me to turn my head again to the ocean, for it seemed as though a memory of what I had seen disturbed me, yet I could not remember what it was. But I could see at once what had affected me, though my eyes had taken no message to my brain when last they saw the surf. It was nearer. It was drawing in. But not only the waves, but the deckchairs also. Swinging my head to the left I found what I expected: the mountains with their pink villas were also approaching – the distance narrowing between the hills and the sea, until it seemed that in a few moments the deckchairs would be among the gardens of the villas, and the things that smoked their pipes, knee-deep in salt water – and the waves splashing their way up and over the neat green lawns and into the parlours of the prawn-coloured houses.

But the road of artificial snow was yet before me, when suddenly the footprints ceased to fly forwards and I was jolted into a spasm of rigidity and silence and the sky came down like a sheet of lead with a yellow circle painted in its centre. And the yellow circle came down with the sky in a dead weight, and striking my head the sun lost all its weight and all its shape for it melted and trickled over my face, and shoulders, a soft petal of fire, like a blob of honey settling into a fold of my sleeve.

And then again the cry of the parrots was heard – 'Amen! Amen! Amen!' and the pages of Deuteronomy fluttered over my face, and as I lowered the lamp, I melted into a dream of tranquil beauty, the white sheets of my bed, as cool as water, swaying about my limbs and sighing 'your journey is over – so wind your watch . . . so wind your watch . . . so wind your watch . . .' and unutterably happy to find myself no longer fast awake I turned over in the great bed and fell wide asleep.

THE INN OF THE FLYING ARSE

Benjamin Péret

I, THE UNDERSIGNED, Benjamin Péret, Certify that these lines were taken down from my dictation, the first section before making love, and the second after.

1. – Before

The man with the wild bollock came down from the tree he had been living in since his first marriage. In each hand he held a sexual organ, from which emerged millions of little larvae which immediately flew off and settled on some large blue flowers. At the larvae's touch, the flowers reared up as if they were made of rubber.

The man was a double male. He advanced toward a rock where a line of vaginas was becoming visible at eye-level. With his finger, he touched one of them, which made a high pitched sound, the second one made an even higher pitched sound, and the third to the touch proved to be as sensitive as an eyebrow. He pressed his thumb on the fourth one with all his might, and the stone gave way. As the stone gave way, two large white arms, and two legs just as white as the arms, appeared and were instantly covered with roses.

The man disappeared, while, in place of the vagina, a long stream of sulphur ran down to the ground. Not far from there, a great yellow flower which was half opened, came off its root, then wound itself around a tree – some kind of magnolia. It stuck itself onto one of the tree's flowers, which then disappeared into its corolla; and a few minutes later, sulphur could be seen dripping from there as well.

From the place where the man disappeared now came the

sound of a propeller turning at full speed, and each second, fragments of bone and flesh emerged from the hole through which the man had entered.

Four flies and two fat spiders started turning silently around the little pile of bone and flesh which itself began to turn as well. Soon a head was formed and then an arm, a leg, a sex, and the entire body of a newborn baby appeared.

The child brought his hand to his sex which was male, the flies and the spiders disappeared through the same hole as the man. The child, his hand on his sex, began to come. The trees, the animals, the rocks began to curl up until they all began to trace the form of a vagina. The child got up, ran to the tree which he tried to grab, but the tree liquefied and poured through his hands, he ran toward the rocks and they flew off.

Once again the child touched his sex with his finger and climaxed. A hedge of male organs came up on either side of him, and the child flew off, followed by two breasts, one white, the other black. He landed some distance away, on the bank of a river; and there he saw emerging from the water the man with the wild bollock, his hands full of excrement which blossomed on contact with the air. A small brain fell with a whistling sound and penetrated the child's skull, ensuring his proper mental development.

The man put the child in his belly, and two Spanish girls threw themselves at his feet, kissing his member with passion. Suddenly, they became round, and took on spots like those of a leopard.

The man stiffened as if he were about to die; the girl who at that moment was licking his member stiffened as well. And the two of them, caught in a propeller-like motion, penetrated an electric cloud and fell at the feet of God.

2. – After

The rug merchant stopped in front of the inn and said: Fresh young girls, nice white little boys! Who wants some, Ladies and Gentlemen?

The man with a fishscale navel, who had one hand on his head, woke up from the long nap he had just taken in the company of a negress: the one he had brought back from a country where the plants move around and make love while walking. He took out his revolver and shot at the merchant, but he had forseen the shot and threw himself to the ground, taking more or less the form of a turtle.

By staring at the electric lights, he started to get drunk. The little star-girl came by, and sold her little perfumed stars to all comers, so she was able to get a meal that evening.

The man with the fishscale navel was again the first to awaken. A dove bearing the olive branch fluttered above his head. He opened the window, the air was pure, the sky was blue, the birds were singing, but all the men were eating in the trees with the hens, and the cocks were in the women's beds.

It was the morning of April 2nd, 1922, and the machines were suffering like women in labour. Only the man who had thrown himself to the ground like a tortoise stretched out his head toward the vulva which he could see a short distance away, but for each forward movement he attempted, the vulva made a corresponding movement further away.

A teal, happening to pass between them, understood their agitation, and consented to stretch itself out in order to link them together. With the tip of its beak pressed to the vulva and one webbed foot on the man's head, the teal turned round and round.

The man with the fishscale navel saw them and burst out laughing, saying:

'You really are gluttons for punishment my poor children.'

THE LAST SUPPER

Jacques Prévert

They sit at table
They eat not
Nor do they touch their plates
Yet their plates stand straight up
Behind their heads.

THE LONDON CASEBOOK OF DETECTIVE RENÉ DESCARTES

Monty Python

CHAPTER 1

T HE ACRID SCENT of stale cigarette smoke hung wearily in the air of the dingy Whitehall office. The only sound was the querulous buzz of a prying bluebottle indolently hopping among the familiar dun box files clustered above the fireplace occupied by the regulation Scotland Yard electric fire, one bar of which flickered hesitantly in a perfunctory attempt to warm the November gloom.

Detective-Inspector René 'Doubty' Descartes absent-mindedly flicked grey-white ash from the sleeve of his only vicuña jacket and stared moodily across the pigeon-violated rooftops of Whitehall. 'I muse,' he thought. 'Therefore . . .'

The ginger telephone shrilled its urgent demand. Descartes, rudely awakened from his reverie, snatched the receiver to his ear.

'Descartes here,' he posited.

'Sorry to interrupt, sir.' The familiar tones of Sergeant Warnock floated down the line. 'Sergeant Warnock here.'

'How can you be sure?'

'I think I am Sergeant Warnock, therefore I am Sergeant Warnock,' replied Sergeant Warnock confidently. Some of Doubty's thinking was beginning to rub off.

'But if you thought you were Marcus Aurelius would you therefore be Marcus Aurelius?' parried the forensic savant deftly.

'Er . . . probably not,' admitted the trusty sergeant, trusting his arm. When the Detective-Inspector was in moods like this, routine business could take days.

'So, simply because you think you are Sergeant Warnock,

it does not necessarily follow that you are,' his postulate continued.

'But, sir, you said, "You think something therefore you are something".'

'No, no, sergeant, you haven't got it at all.'

'Well, sir,' the stalwart sergeant gamely countered, 'there must be a strong probability that I am Sergeant Warnock. Couldn't we on this occasion proceed on that assumption.'

'I'm afraid that it is this "beyond all reasonable doubt" philosophy that has bedevilled the reputation of police thinking since the days of that woolly pragmatist Peel.'

'But this is an urgent matter, sir. The Prime Minister is on the other line.'

'My dear putative sergeant, this problem of your identity is something we are going to have to sort out sooner or later.'

'But it's the *Prime Minister*, sir.'

'But how do we *know* that it is the Prime Minister?'

'Oh Christ.'

'This is a perfect illustration of my theme, Warnock . . .'

'Aha!'

'. . . if that is indeed to whom I am speaking. If I cannot be sure of the Warnockness of the person or apparent person with whom I am at present speaking, how *a fortiori* can I accept an authentication from this source of a third party of whom my direct and verifiable experience is even further removed?'

'He's rung off anyway, sir.'

'If indeed he was ever there.'

'Well if he was, sir, then he almost definitely asked you to call him back. Can I get him for you, sir?'

'Not so fast, sergeant, for I will assume for the moment that that is who you are.'

'Thank you very much, sir.'

'If I now call the Prime Minister, how is he for certain to know that he is speaking to *me*?'

'Ah but that's *his* problem, sir.'

'But how shall I know that I am speaking to *him*?'

'You're calling him, sir.'

'But suppose I speak to someone, thinking him to be the Prime Minister when in fact he is not, *then* the Prime Minister will be disclosing what may well be state secrets to another party, believing him to be me.'

'But surely, sir, just because you're speaking to a third party it does not follow as a necessary consequence that the P.M. is speaking to anyone at all.'

Descartes sucked thoughtfully at his familiar thumb. '. . . Good work, sergeant. Get him *toute suite*.' Then replacing the receiver he ruefully swung round on the familiar leather trapeze and stared wistfully out of the window. 'Funny old London,' he thought. At least the pouring rain had stopped. Or rather, it certainly seemed there was no entity *a*, such that '*x* is rainy and pouring' was true when *x* was *a*, but not otherwise.

CHAPTER 2

The door of Number Ten shut and he found himself once again in the oddly unpleasant driving sleet and hail to which his fourteen years in London had still not accustomed him. Setting off briskly across the street, dodging the swishing taxis, he hurried towards the warm and beckoning portals of New Scotland Yard. Why was it, he mused, that the Prime Minister always lost his temper with him? How could the P.M. become so agitated about a country whose very existence had never been properly established? Let alone the intentions of its supposed inhabitants to obtain what the Prime Minister had persisted in referring to as 'secrets'. 'Relative secrets' Doubty could have accepted subject only to a few minor qualifications but his attempts to point out this terminological slackness had received alarming rebuffs from the Prime Minister, a man at the best of times inclined to leap to unsatisfactorily substantiated conclusions, but on this occasion made positively foolhardy by the presence of a man he clearly believed to be the President of the United States of America, on no better evidence, as far as Doubty could deduce, than an exact but superficial physical resemblance to the man normally referred to by the American people as the President, the presence of a couple of hundred alleged 'bodyguards', a so-called Vice-President and a small cavalcade. The last three items, as he had dutifully pointed out, could have been easily faked by a reasonably competent organiser and were in no way contingent upon the Presidentness of the Nixon-like person, while the appearance of the latter, although at first sight impressive to the untrained mind, was still explicable in terms of a twin, a 'double', a highly sophisticated working model, an ordinary optical illusion occurring simultaneously to the apparent Prime Minister and himself, a hallucination caused by the possible presence of certain substances in the Downing Street tea, or, and this was the possibility that Doubty had found increasingly attractive, an oleograph. And it was after all in an attempt to discount this last suspicion that he had struck the putative oleograph the light blow across the top of the head that had caused all the trouble. But why, mused a curious Doubty as he absent-mindedly picked slivers of Prime Ministerial telephone from his scalp, should he now be sent to Tonga in the guise of an ordinary police constable and for an unspecified length of time?

Was *this* to be the Big One?

CHAPTER 3

The acrid scent of stale coconut milk hung wearily in the air of the sun-drenched Tongan beach. The only sound was the insistent lapping of the prying waves indolently hopping among the familiar dun rock piles clustered about the bay occupied by the regulation Tongan Government-issue catamaran, one float of which glistened hesitantly in a perfunctory attempt to out-shine the August glare.

Police Constable René 'Doubty' Descartes absent-mindedly flicked the familiar coconut shells from the sleeve of his only vicuña swimming trunks and stared pointlessly across the crab-befouled beaches of White-bay. 'I stare pointlessly,' he thought, 'therefore I . . .' But his reverie was rudely interrupted by the sharp gurgle of a passing flying fish and turning on his familiar heel he picked his way briskly through the swirling lobsters towards the beckoning head of the beach and the equally beckoning cool of the familiar majestic New Reichenbach Falls so many feet above his head and slightly to one side.

As he mounted the ginger path leading to the bridge which so precariously straddled the churning, tumultuous uproar of this watery object, he mentally summarised the past fourteen months.

'Not much, really,' he opined to himself, 'Very little paper-work; very little paper; none at all actually; which is why I am summarizing my thoughts mentally.' Pleased with this conclusion he strode perfunctorily through the driving sunshine past the enchanting pink-shuttered office of the cheery waterfall-keeper, hardly noticing the cluster of blazing bouganivillea just beyond, that reminds one so strongly of the cluster of blazing bouganivillea that one sees just outside Harry's bar, at the corner of Victoria Street and A. A. Milne Crescent, in the main square of Tonga's sleepy capital Tongatapu, where I have been, as you can tell from this description.

By now P.C. Descartes had cautiously stepped out on to the unfamiliar wildly swaying bakelite footbridge which alone stood between him and a watery grave with some bits of rock in it. Staring down into the frothy cascading vortex he nonchalantly flicked the familiar ice-cold spume from his navy-blue vicuña helmet. 'I muse,' he mused, 'therefore I am about to be interrup–'

But his muse was interrupted by the lisping bark he had somehow half-expected.

'Good morning.' Edward de Bono, his arch enemy, and

notoriously lateral thinker stood on the bridge, in a mysterious sideways position. 'Good morning,' he rasped angrily. No response . . . 'Good morning,' he re-rasped fiercely, mentally sidling a little. The bakelite bridge seemed to rattle the more violently in reply. Descartes stood his bakelite and mused on the awesome de Bono's existence with all the power he could muster. De Bono, seeing the familiar tell-tale beads of sweat stand out on Doubty's forehead sensed victory. 'Snap!' the bakelite seemed to muse, and a second later, moving laterally, sent the two combatants in an unexpected direction and a probably watery grave respectively.

'A long way down,' the inspector commented inwardly, disbelieving de Bono's existence to the last as he apparently plummeted.

'Somewhere in the distance one could hear the faint familiar cry of an eloping litter-bin,' yelled de Bono, thinking laterally to the last. There was a sickening crash, followed by a sickening cry, then two sickening splashes, a sickening crunch and then three sickening noises that are very difficult to describe.

'So . . . I am dead,' thought Doubty. 'Wait a minute . . . I'm thinking . . . I think, therefore I. . . .'

With one logical bound he was.

¡Scandal!

THE TROJAN HORSE

Raymond Queneau

A MAN CAME into the café, and there was a mist. He installed himself at the bar, hoisting himself on to a stool, which conjured up the appearance of a bar-tender in a white jacket and with a ferocious look. All the tables were occupied, and the people thereat were minding their own business. The waiters were yawning. The newcomer had a good look round – no, there wasn't a single place free. So he answered the question his adversary had just put to him.

'I'll have a glass of water,' he said.

'Very good, sir,' replied the barman.

He examined the individual with respect and set to work. He took a big beer glass, sent a piece of ice spinning round in it, flung away the iceberg in disgust, engaged a jug of water, placed the misted glass on the counter, put the receptacle adjacent to it.

'There you are, sir,' said he, this man.

The other poured himself a glass of water and drank a little. Then he sat still, miles away. The people at the tables, men and women, were minding their own business. The barman had become immersed in other exertions. It was cold outside. The hands of the clock on the wall, electric at that, metaphysically chased each other. The nice plump cashier was dozing.

The man took the glass between his hands and again sipped a little water. The orchestra embarked on a waltz tune. A few people got up and embracing each other described complicated curves on the ground. The barman surreptitiously knocked back a bloody big gulp of gin. A newspaper-seller came in, then went out, overwhelmed by the bloodiness of the world, real or transcribed. The hands had just met on the clockface, which happens frequently every day. At last the door opened again and a woman came in.

She immediately located the man she was looking for and sat down beside him. The barman hove in sight.

'I'll have another glass of water,' said the man. 'This one's got tepid.'

'You wouldn't like mineral water this time?'

'No,' replied the man.

'And for the lady?' asked the barman.

'Nothing,' replied the woman.

'And will that be all for today?' asked the barman, with only mild insolence.

'Yes,' said the man, 'that'll be all.'

The barman served the second glass of water. He put a piece of ice in it.

'Well?' the woman asked the man.

'Well, nothing, what a life,' murmured the man.

'It isn't funny,' said the woman.

She had a look round.

A character with glasses was dancing with a prostitute, doing fancy steps for the benefit of the gallery and smiling for the benefit of the pianist. He looked a bit drunk and not altogether at his ease.

'A cashier who's skipped with the till,' said the man.

'Think so?' said the woman.

'Yes, it's obvious.'

A few characters were dancing with their hats on.

'It's amusing here,' said the man.

'Yes,' said the woman.

The music stopped and the violinist waved his instrument about at arm's length while conversing with a woman who was alone at her table. The dancers went back to their tables. The cashier did so with exhibitionism. A horse who happened to be sitting at the bar leant over and asked the woman if she'd like to have a drink with him, likewise the gentleman accompanying her.

'What does he want?' said the man. 'Does he want you to dance with him?'

'No,' murmured the woman, 'I think he wants us to have a drink with him.'

The horse had got down from his stool and was bowing to them, making sweeping gestures with his forelegs. He had some difficulty in finding his words.

'You,' he explained, 'you, both, you have a drink with me.'

The man gave him a bored look.

'No thank you,' he said coldly.

The horse didn't seem to feel quite in his element. The woman was a little terrified. The man asked her how her Aunt Charlotte was. She was very important for them, Aunt Charlotte was. But it embarrassed the woman to talk about her in front of the horse, about Aunt Charlotte. She jibbed. The horse waited, patiently however, until they had finished their little aside. Handsomely greased by the cashier on the spree, the orchestra had resumed their labours and broken into a pot-pourri of waltzes, 1900. The horse waved its big legs about and taking advantage of a gap in the conversation relative to Aunt Charlotte, pronounced these words:

'Perhaps you think I'm drunk? Certainly not, certainly not, certainly not.'

He scanned these words, prancing about gracefully. Then he looked at them, rolling terrible eyes. He was a great big hack, black all over, somewhat gaunt, with nicely polished hoofs and a corkscrewed tail tied with a purple ribbon.

'No no, I'm not drunk, but I can't always control my movements, my remarks, my words, my . . .'

He seemed to be thinking:

'My conversations. I need to . . . I need to . . .'

He seemed to be thinking:

'To adapt myself. Yes, that's it – to adapt myself.'

He gave them a broad grin which revealed a set of strong, yellowish teeth, in the interstices of which, here and there, bits of hay could be seen.

'To adapt myself,' he resumed complacently.

'He's absolutely tight,' the man murmured.

'You haven't got a cigarette have you?' the woman asked him, taking no notice of the horse. 'I've forgotten mine.'

The man held out a packet of Gauloises to her. But the horse, speedily thrusting a hoof into his saddle pocket, extirpated from it a box bedizened with red and gold. He opened it. It contained bits of straw twisted and plaited into the shape of cigarillos. He offered one to the woman.

'They must be revolting,' murmured the woman.

'Don't let yourself be bullied,' the man advised her discreetly.

'No thank you,' said the woman, 'I prefer Gauloises.'

The horse turned towards the man, who refused.

'Me too. Anyway, I never smoke after nine in the evening.'

The horse looked at them suspiciously. They smiled politely at him. The woman lit her Gauloise. The man lit nothing. The horse swished his tail from side to side. Finally he put the box back in his saddle pocket. At this moment the cashier on the spree fell on his bottom and the waiters started to throw paper streamers about, trying to look as if they were enjoying themselves.

'Don't you think,' said the man, 'that we could try and touch Aunt Charlotte?'

'She's so mean,' said the woman.

'All the same, in our position.'

'You try,' said the woman. 'She likes you.'

'Yes I know she does. What a bore. What a life.'

The horse was waiting solemnly till they'd finished. After this last interjection he judged the moment ripe to intervene.

'I've got an aunt, too,' he said shrewdly. 'And you'll have a drink with me,' he added, in a more threatening manner.

'What a,' the man began, but he interrupted himself to drink a mouthful of water.

'Are you a Houyhnhnm,' asked the woman pleasantly.

This question seemed to delight the horse. He again started

waving his great legs about, and rolling his eyes.

'Not Houyhnhnm,' he neighed. 'Not Houyhnhnm. Not Houyhnhnm at all. Guess?'

He leant over towards them, as if they were a peck of oats. Or even two. His eyes were shining.

'Not Houyhnhnm,' he insisted. 'Guess?'

Confronted with this mystery, the man and the woman didn't know what to answer.

'When could we go and see her?' the man asked the woman.

'No no,' exclaimed the horse, with a benevolent smile. 'Not speak other things. Guess.'

'Houyhnhnm,' said the man resignedly.

'No no, not Houyhnhnm, not Houyhnhnm.'

'Then we don't know,' said the man resignedly.

The horse's smile became more and more paternal.

'Come on. Just try. A famous town. Guess. Guess.'

'Bloody bore he is,' said the man between his teeth.

But the horse was still smiling benevolently, and was still showing them his; his teeth.

The woman had a shot.

'Auteuil?'

'No,' exclaimed the horse, absolutely delighted with this little game.

'Le Tremblay?'

'No no.'

'Chantilly?'

'No no no.'

She enumerated other racecourses. But it was still no.

In the end, finishing his glass of water, the man said to the horse:

'We don't know.'

And to the woman:

'Aren't you thirsty? Don't you want a glass of water?'

'With me. I want you to have a drink with me,' declared the horse authoritatively. 'We'll come back to that in a minute. Then you not know? I mean: you don't know?'

'No,' said the woman.

'Well then, I come from Troy.'

'Ah!' said the others.

'I'm Trojan,' insisted the nag.

'Ah, Trojan,' said the others.

'Yes, I comefm Troy,' neighed the horse, at the highest pitch of excitement.

'He's not drunk,' said the man, 'he's doped.'

'What's more,' said the horse from Troy, 'I'm going to show you my pedigree.'

He flung one of his forelegs behind him and rummaged in his saddle pockets. He pulled out a filthy notebook and started turning over its pages feverishly. Some pages looked as if they were stained with horse-dung.

'You see, eh, I was born in Troy. But Dad was born in Saratoga, and Mother in Epsom. They both had two hoofs. Mean to say, each one two hoofs. But I have some ancestors who had four.'

'No?' said the man, dubiously.

He turned towards the barman and ordered two glasses of water.

'You'll be broke again tomorrow,' said the woman.

'And will that be all for today?' asked the barman.

'Yes,' said the man.

'Stop, stop!' said the horse to the barman. 'I'm inviting them to a drink.'

The barman hesitated.

'You can give us a glass of water for two all the same,' said the man.

'Yes yes,' said the horse, 'we'll have a drink together in a minute, but me still one thing to ask, you guess. I mean: I still have one question to ask you.'

'Go ahead,' said the man, with a yellow and martyred look which spread all over his face, starting from the corner of his mouth.

The horse put his pedigree back in his saddle pocket and took out his smokable hay.

'No? You don't want to smoke?'

'No,' said the man and the woman in chorus.

He slipped a cigarillo between two teeth and held it up to the barman's lighter. He took a few puffs at it which he projected towards the ceiling. His face grew calmer, his eyes seemed to betray a certain satisfaction. And even some pretension. He started to speak again as follows:

'You'll certainly never guess my profession.'

'Perhaps you go in for sports?' suggested the woman, diffidently.

'I do, a little, from time to time,' replied the horse, placidly. 'I race, it's true, now and then, but only in gentlemen's races. No, that's not it. I'm a student.'

'Of botany?' asked the man, trying to force himself into irrationality.

'Not bad, not bad,' replied the horse importantly. 'No, of genetics.'

'Of what?' asked the woman.

Suddenly interested, the barman tried to join in the conversation.

'You're interested in genetics, sir?' he said to the horse.

'Precisely.'

There was a short interval. The musicians were tucking in to some refreshments. The cashier on the spree had finally collapsed into the arms of a woman of easy virtue. A slight hubbub was all that betrayed the intellectual life of those present.

The horse was surrounded with a sort of bored respect. This gave him great satisfaction. He started to hold forth:

'Yes,' he said, 'it's a science that particularly concerns my family. Just imagine.'

He made a reconnaissance with his big eyes to see if they were really listening.

'Just imagine,' he continued, 'that grandpa was a centaur and grandma was a mare. And so, according to Mendelian laws, here's the result.'

He patted himself on the breast with his hoofs somewhat pedantically.

'But,' he added proudly, 'I have a sister who has two hoofs. She's a night-club dancer.'

He smiled knowingly.

'She's often to be seen in the tableau entitled *The Fight of the Amazons*.'

He took his time and sent a puff of smoke towards the ceiling.

'She takes the part of a little horse.'

Another pause.

'It's just one of life's little ironical touches,' he concluded.

The barman roared with laughter, delighted.

The man and the woman tried to grin.

'Nothing like keeping you hanging around for it,' grumbled the man under his breath.

The acute ear of the barman grasped the allusion. He asked brightly:

'Well, what's it going to be, ladies and gents?'

'That's right, that's right,' neighed the horse, again starting to gesticulate wildly with his forelegs. 'A drink. I'm standing you a drink.'

'What would you like?' the man asked the woman.

The woman hesitated for a moment.

'A gin fizz,' she finally said.

'A gin fizz for the lady,' the barman confirmed with growing enthusiasm.

'Me too – a gin fizz,' said the man.

'And for you, sir?' the barman asked the horse.

'Gin fizz,' said the horse.

'That'll be three gin fizzes,' bawled the barman.

He swooped down on his appliances while the orchestra attacked a new selection of tunes, 1900, in answer to the general demand of the felt-hatted dancers.

'You're right,' the woman said to the man, 'there's nothing else we can do. You'll have to go and touch Aunt Charlotte.'

'I'll go tomorrow,' said the man. 'But it isn't funny.'

'And how old would you say I was?' the horse asked them.

They turned their heads towards him.

'Forty,' said the woman dully.

'You're crazy,' said the man in a low voice. 'At that age he wouldn't be a horse, he'd be a carcass.'

He turned towards the horse.

'No,' he said. 'Two and a half, three.'

'Precisely,' said the horse with satisfaction.

Then his expression suddenly changed and became quite frigid.

'But,' he asked the man, 'why you say carcass?'

'Me?' replied the man, with a falsely innocent air.

'Yes, you,' said the horse. 'Why you say carcass?'

'Oh! yes,' said the man airily. 'Carcass. Carcass.'

'Yes, carcass,' said the horse.

He started waving his forelegs about and then suddenly lashed out energetically at nobody in particular. The dancers moved away respectfully.

'Carcass,' he neighed, 'you said carcass.'

'I was talking about Aunt Charlotte,' said the man.

'Yes, of course,' exclaimed the woman. 'We were talking about Aunt Charlotte just now.'

'Who's sure to die soon,' added the man.

They started to laugh knowingly.

The horse seemed to have calmed down. He now looked at them with a severe and oval eye.

'Here's your three gin fizzes, ladies and gents,' said the barman, putting the glasses down in front of the customers.

'No,' said the horse.

With a deft, yet dignified, touch of the hoof, he slid the other two gin fizzes in front of his.

'The three for me,' he said to the barman.

He turned calmly and majestically towards the two friends.

'Aunt Charlotte,' the man explained, 'is sure to die soon.'

The horse didn't answer.

'Anyway he's a bloody bore,' the man said to the woman. 'Come on.'

They got down from their stools.

'Goodnight,' said the barman impartially.

'Goodnight,' they replied.

They stopped when they got to the door.

It had started to snow.

'You'll get your feet wet again,' said the man.

'Oh well,' said the woman.

They turned round and saw the horse who had already drunk two of the gin fizzes. The horse pretended not to see them. He started to drink the third. With a straw.

They went out.

'Stinking weather,' said the man.

'Don't get excited,' said the woman.

'Tomorrow I'll go and touch Aunt Charlotte,' said the man.

PHONETIC POEM

Man Ray

MAN RAY
Paris, Mai 1924

203

THE INDIAN ROPE TRICK
EXPLAINED

Rudy Rucker

PARIS WAS BACKWARDS. Charlie Raumer sat on a patch of grass near the Louvre trying to straighten it out. The kids were fighting, Cybele wasn't speaking to him, and all around was the mirror-image of the Paris he remembered from twelve years ago.

He buried his face in his hands, pushing at the misty red memories. He imagined a Paris made of glass, a relief map. If you looked at it from the wrong side, everything would be backwards, inside-out. He began tugging at the surfaces in his image to put them right. Something began . . . there was a heavy thud on his back.

It was Iris, the ten-year-old. 'What's the matter, Daddy, are you *drunk?*' She broke into a wild giggle at this sally, and her two little brothers joined in, pigs at the party. They piled onto his back with a confused squealing. Someone shrieked, 'POKE!' and little Jimmy fell crying to the ground.

Raumer's teeth clenched. 'Iris, you stop it or . . .'

'It was Howard,' she yelled with a grimace at the larger of her two little brothers. Distrusting speech, Howard charged her, arms windmilling. Raumer seized the two and shook them hard. Their little faces looked crooked and ugly.

'Stop, stop, *stop!*' It was Cybele, back with a precious paper bag of postcards. When she was a girl she had spent every Sunday in the Louvre. But now that she was finally here again, her family had refused to come inside.

'Mine, Mama. Me.' Jimmy took an uncertain step forwards. Howard snaked past him and snatched the cards from his mother. Iris cross-checked Howard and they hit the ground together.

Raumer dealt out two back-handed slaps and recovered the cards. The printing on the museum shop bag was reversed. He wished he had never started fooling with the Hinton hypercube models.

'Is that all you can do?' his wife was demanding, an orchid of anger blossoming in her voice. '*Beat* them? Why don't you ever *help* me instead of *ruining* our . . .'

All this time a part of Raumer's mind had been fiddling with his image of Paris. Now instead of trying to make it come right he let it *be* backward, let himself go. He felt a rush of freedom. And disappeared.

He snapped back on the steps of the Louvre, thirty meters away. Nothing looked backwards anymore. In a twinkling instant the two heavily ornamented wings of the building had changed places. His tailbone hurt where he'd dropped onto the steps. Across the road he could see Cybele and the kids looking for him.

'*Bhom bhom bho-la?*'

Raumer turned. A tall African was hunkering just behind him. A street-vendor. They were all over Paris this June. White plastic ivory elephants, brittle leather belts, strangely patterned wallets, and the little drums mounted on sticks. The vendor was twirling one of the drums between his fingers. There were two clay marbles attached with string, and when the drum twirled, the marbles rattled on the taut skins.

'*Bhom bhom bho-la?*'

'*Non merci. Pas acheter.*' As he tried to brush the peddler off, the utter strangeness of what had just happened was hitting Raumer. He had been over there, and now he was here. Had he blacked out? But there was nothing stronger than coffee and a hangover in his system. Across the road, Iris squealed and pointed up at him.

'*Je vous le donne,*' the African said, holding out the little drum. Still twirling it. Pattapattapattapat. '*Pour devenir sauteur.*' Serious eyes under a high, noble forehead.

Raumer took the drum. *For becoming a jumper.* So the African had seen. Raumer had really jumped thirty meters. But . . .

Iris came pumping up the steps, her eyes fixed on the toy. 'Can it be mine, Dad?'

A light touch of long fingers on Raumer's shoulder. '*Inquirez devant le Centre Pompidou.*' He turned to thank, to ask, but the tall African was already gliding down the steps, no leg-movements visible under his black and yellow *dashiki.*

Iris was tugging at the drum now. One of the little clay marbles came off and bounced down the steps. Raumer bared his teeth at the child, then retrieved the ball. He slipped it into his coat pocket with the drum before the others could start in.

'You didn't have to run *off* like that,' Cybele said, looking not quite pleased to have found him. 'We didn't even see you cross the *street.*'

'Daddy bought a toy drum, and it's mine,' Iris announced. Jimmy's face quivered, and Howard stepped forward, alert eyes fixed on the bulge in Raumer's pocket.

'*What is the matter with you children?*' Cybele demanded. 'Can't you stop asking for things for one *minute?*'

'I'll get them each a drum,' Raumer muttered. Four of the Africans were standing in a group ten meters away. Impassively, with long arcing gestures, they were working a stream of Canadian tourists. They could have been catching fish. Raumer hesitated, trying to decide which one he had talked with.

'You will *not,*' Cybele said, taking his arm. An old lady had just stepped out of a cab and onto the curb next to them. Cybele called to the cab driver in rapid French, then herded Raumer in. 'I am going to *feed* you and these children before you *murder* each other.'

Raumer had a veal cutlet with a fried egg on it; Cybele had calf-brains in brown butter; and the kids each had a little steak with *pommes frites*. Coffee, apple juice, wine . . . they were all smiling at each other. A cool June day in Paris. It's ridiculous what a difference food makes. The kids drifted across the cheap restaurant to play pinball with two francs they had scrounged.

Raumer took the toy drum out of his pocket to tie the string Iris had snapped. 'So you *did* buy one,' Cybele said, lighting a cigarette. 'It's cute.'

'One of those Africans gave it to me,' Raumer said. 'For jumping thirty meters through hyperspace.'

'What are you talking about?'

'I figure that's what happened. When I disappeared. I'd been having that mirror-image feeling again and . . .'

Cybele sighed a cloud of smoke. 'This is our *vacation*, Charlie. Our last chance. Can't you just wait till you're back in your library to be *so crazy*?' She tried to soften the last word with a strained smile.

'I don't think it's crazy to be writing a book on the history of the fourth dimension. What am I supposed to do . . . walk around holding your hand as if we were still courting?'

'It might be nice.' Suddenly her reserve broke. 'Oh, Charlie, don't you *care*? We fell in *love* here. And if now all we can do is . . . *fight* . . . then we're . . .' She held a supplicating hand out across the table.

'My jumping like that fits in with the theory I found in the Hinton book,' Raumer said slowly, not really noticing his wife. 'We have a slight thickness in the fourth dimension. We're like coins sliding around on a table-top. Our consciousness is down with the table-top . . . but if you somehow identify with the *top* side of the coin then things look backwards. At the Louvre I finally let myself go all the way up. The momentum flipped me right off the board. I could have come down anywhere. I could have come down backwards or sideways . . .'

While he talked, Raumer twirled the carved rod sticking out of the little tom-tom's side. The strings and weights followed along, trailing like a galaxy's spiral arms. When he reversed direction, the little marbles pattered on the tight skins. He rolled the stick back and forth, getting the hang of it. Pattapat. Pattapattapat.

'You don't . . . you don't really . . .' Cybele began, then gave up. 'Why don't we all rest and then go see the Pompidou Art Center at Beaubourg?' she suggested in a changed, artificially bright voice. 'I hear it's the kind of place where you and the kids won't get bored.'

A wail cut the air. Howard. Iris had pushed the reset button on the pinball machine, and Howard's franc had been lost. Raumer went over to put in another coin.

The machine was called *Dimension Warp*. The glass scoreboard carried a bright picture of two women learning the ropes from a hyperspace pilot who's a robot. Those naughty cuties are taking notes and licking the points of their thick pencils . . . while that jivey robobopster fingers the controls. The player as machine, courting curvy Nature. Groovy.

Raumer split three games with Iris and Howard. Jimmy got to pull the plunger. The machine had an unusual feature, a little ramp a ball could jump over to land somewhere else on the board . . . in a special and otherwise inaccessible freegame hole if you were lucky. The cover-glass was set up high enough so the ball could sail quite a distance before clacking back into the plane of normal play.

'That's what you did, Daddy,' Howard said the first time the ball made its trip through the third dimension.

'What do you mean?' Raumer gave his son a sharp look. He couldn't always tell what went on behind that smooth seven-year-old forehead.

'He means that your turn's over,' Iris interjected. They left it at that.

Their hotel was nearby, and Cybele wanted to go up to rest and change shoes. Little Jimmy needed a nap and Iris wanted to keep an eye on her mother. Eager to avoid the possibility of another ugly scene in the tiny hotel room, Raumer proposed that he kill some time with Howard and meet the others in front of the Pompidou Center in an hour and a half. Cheerfully, father and son boarded the Metro.

In between stations the Dubonnet ads flickered past. DUBO . . . DUBON . . . DUBONNET . . . DUBO . . . DUBON . . . DUBONNET . . . Over and over. A pun. *Du beau*: lovely; *du bon*: tasty. Cybele had explained it to him the first time he'd come to Paris. Twelve years now. She'd been an art student then and he'd been at the *Université* on a scholars exchange program. An American machine courting a French cutie. Somehow he'd won her. But now he only wondered why he'd wanted to.

'What if the ball went under the board like a subway?' Howard asked suddenly, his big opened eyes reflecting in the black glass.

Cybele had told Raumer about Howard's long ruminations. 'All the machinery, the electrical stuff, is under the board,' he smiled. 'The ball would probably get stuck, half under and half over.'

He had a sudden impulse to talk to the boy, to teach him something. He hardly knew the child, really. In the normal run of things Cybele did all the work with the children.

'Imagine this, Howard. Imagine that there were pictures that could slide around just on the pinball board. What would the ball look like to them when it rolled around?'

'Like a ball.'

'No, dummy. If all they could see was what touched their plane, then the ball would look like a dot moving around.'

'Unless you pushed it through.'

'That's right. If you pushed the ball through the plane they'd see a circular cross-section. And when the ball jumps off the ramp, they'd think it had disappeared.'

'Why do you call it a cross-section. Cross means X.'

'It can mean cutting, too. If I had a real big sharp knife I could make a cross-section of you . . . cut you down the middle and shave off a nice thin . . .' Raumer stopped himself. That was no way to talk to a child. What was the matter with him?

At the next stop they had to change trains. Raumer's memory was still playing tricks on him . . . they caught their connecting train in the wrong direction. Upset, he yelled at Howard for wanting to go to the bathroom.

When they finally got to the right stop, the boy's face had turned into a tight little mask. Raumer suddenly realized that no one in his family really liked him. They had no reason to. Trying to buy a smile, he gave Howard the toy drum. No reaction. They climbed the stairs, and stepped out into the plaza next to the *Centre Pompidou*.

The building itself is as wonderful as anything in it. It is built inside-out, with all the structural supports, heating shafts, escalators, plumbing and electrical conduits attached to the outside walls. The machinery is all outside, and the traditional decoration is all hanging on the walls inside. The marvelous joke is that a lot of those functional-looking pipes outside are fake . . . pure this-is-not-a-decoration decoration. It isn't enough for the building to *be* inside-out, it has to *look* inside out.

The plaza was dotted with idlers, many of them arranged into circles around street-performers: a juggler, a fire-eater lying on a mound of broken glass, and a crazy man shouting fifty years too late about *rayons ultraviolets*. The chilly breeze was snatching the words out of people's mouths and scattering them around the big square.

Right by the subway stairs there were a few sidewalk artists waiting for people to drop coins onto the pastels they'd drawn on the stone ground. One of the artists had filled in the black outline of a boy with fanciful pictures of body organs and thoughts.

Howard begged till Raumer put half a franc on the man's picture, and then he pulled his father over to join a group watching a snake-charmer. Snakers are supposed to be Indian, but this charmer was another of the *dashiki*-clad Africans.

He was squatting on a piece of cloth patterned with squares and slanting lines. His snakes writhed sluggishly and spilled out of a big wicker basket. His flute was a gourd with two pipes sticking out. One pipe had holes for fingering the eerie, wandering notes, and the other led air out to play on the face of the snake being charmed.

A cobra on the basket top weaved back and forth, following the movements of the snaker's flute. Its hood was spread menacingly, and occasionally it made as if to strike. The tune drifted up and down a pentatonic scale, weaving like the snake's body. Little Howard began twirling his drum in accompaniment. Typically, he'd been able to play it as soon as Raumer gave it to him.

When the snaker heard the sound of the pattering, his eyes flashed at them. The tune speeded up, and Howard kept pace. Slowly the snaker rose to a crouch, drawing the cobra higher and higher. Finally he was standing erect on his long legs and the cobra had reared up to an impossible height. Raumer hoped its venom sacs were gone. The music cut off abruptly and the cobra collapsed back to a great, shifting coil.

'*Bhom bhom bho-la!*' the African shouted. He was an imposing man with stiff ebony features. A few coins pattered onto the tessellated cloth beneath his feet. '*Dix francs de plus et je vous montre une merveille!*' He held out his ten fingers. He wanted more money.

Perhaps this was the man he'd been told to see, Raumer thought. That African by the Louvre had said something about coming here. On a sudden impulse he fingered a limp bill out of his pocket and tossed it onto the snaker's cloth. Ten francs. It seemed like play-money.

'*Merci, Monsieur de l'Espace,*' the tall black man said with a slight bow. '*Et maintenant! Le truc indien!*' He whistled sharply, penetratingly, and a young African boy in shorts came running across the square, carrying a heavy coiled rope.

The snaker gave a longer speech then, but Raumer couldn't follow it. What had the man called him? *Monsieur de l'Espace?*

He couldn't figure it out. What a strange day this was. First that funny gap or jump near the Louvre . . . and now this snake charmer was making a *rope* uncoil and slowly rise into the air.

Howard was tugging his sleeve; he had something to say. 'There's a thread attached to the rope,' came the deafening whisper. 'The little boy is pulling it up.'

The kid was right. Sharp-eyed little devil. There was a grey thread leading up from the rope. The thread looped over a nail in the air overhead, and the little assistant was surreptitiously reeling the thread in behind his back. Ten francs for such a cheap . . . a nail in the air?

The music squeaked, rose higher, and disappeared into the supersonic. The snaker laid down his flute. The end of the rope was up at the nail . . . it looked more like a thorn, really. With a single precise gesture, the African reached up and attached the rope to the thorn.

Meanwhile the little boy was sitting on the cube-patterned cloth, binding a long thorn lengthwise to the bottom of each foot. The thorns stuck out in front like crampons.

'*Dix francs,*' the snaker cried, pacing back and forth with his long fingers outspread. '*Seulement dix francs de plus et mon fils va monter!*'

Quite a crowd had gathered now. Raumer and Howard were in the front row, but the people were three deep behind them. A few coins flew through the air and landed near the snakes. The cobra struck half-heartedly at a twenty-centime piece. The little boy was ready now, a thorn sticking out past the toes of each foot, and a third thorn clasped ice-pick style in his right hand.

'*Encore trois francs!*' the father shouted after looking things over. '*Encore trois!*' One more franc piece landed on the cloth. And then nothing. They all waited. The breeze grew colder. Where was the sun? This was supposed to be June.

'Lend me two francs, Daddy,' Howard whispered. It looked like no one else was going to cough up. With a sigh Raumer fished his last two coins out. All his family ever wanted from him was money.

Howard trotted over and handed the coins to the snaker. The man's hand whipped out and caught Howard by the wrist. He took the little drum from him, and then leaned over and whispered something. Raumer stepped forward, but Howard was already free. The snaker had given him a straw-wrapped package in place of the drum. He skipped back, his eyebrows high with excitement.

The music started up again. The snaker was playing the flute with one hand and the drum with the other. His mouth remained fixed in the same mask-like expression. The little black boy made a stroboscopic series of gestures and began to climb.

He held the rope with his left hand only. Foot by foot, hand by hand, he worked himself into the air. He would pull a foot loose, then set the thorn with a sharp kick. Slide the left hand up, reset the right hand, reset the feet. It was like watching a mountain climber kicking ice-steps for himself in a steep snow-field.

When the boy reached the top of the rope he began pulling the rope up after him. The crowd was absolutely silent. The music wailed and pattered, the flute-tone flowing over the beats like a stream over round stones.

The boy had the rope coiled over his left shoulder now. Holding himself steady with his right hand, he pulled loose the thorn that had held the rope. He reset it at shoulder level and paused, pressed against the aether like a tree-fog on a windowpane. His thin, wooden-looking limbs tensed.

Suddenly the boy was gone. The audience broke into a wild hubbub of cheers and questions. Coins rained onto the African's cloth. He bowed once and began gathering up his snakes. The show was over. People drifted off.

'*There* you are. We looked all *over*.'

'What did you buy for Howard? What's he got in his hand?'

'Dada!'

Raumer turned with a smile. 'We just saw the most incredible thing. This kid climbed up a rope, pulled it up after him and disappeared. The Indian Rope Trick! I've read about it for years. And now I understand how it works. I've got to ask that guy where the bush . . .'

But when he turned back the snaker had disappeared, faded into the crowd, basket and all. Meanwhile Iris had unwrapped Howard's package.

'Four stickers!' she exclaimed. 'Good for *poking!*'

'Let me see those.' Raumer scooped the long, reddish thorns up. Testing, he jabbed one in the air. It dug in and stuck in something invisible.

'What are you *teaching* the children, Charlie? They could put each other's *eyes* out that way. Throw those things *away!*'

Raumer released the thorn cautiously. It stayed fixed in the air where he'd jabbed it. Wonderingly, he looked at the tips of the other three. The tips seemed to bend . . . yet not bend. They weren't quite fully there.

'These are thorns from the legendary bush of *Shanker Bhola*, Cybele. Aether pitons. I always thought it was only a . . .' Raumer sat down on the pavement and unlaced a shoe. 'It's as if those coins on the table had little needles to dig into the wood. Then they wouldn't have to just slide wherever the forces pulled them. They'd be free to climb against gravity through empty space.'

Raumer had both shoes off now. He laid one of the long thorns inside each shoe and pushed them forward, through the leather. They stuck out the front like toe-spurs. He began lacing the shoes back on, his feet squeezed in over the thornshafts.

'What's Daddy doing?'

'*I* don't know, Iris. I don't know *what's* the matter with your father.'

'He wants to climb through the air like the little black boy,' Howard explained. 'Those thorns can stick in the air.'

A few passers-by had gathered to watch Raumer putting his shoes on. *'Dix francs!'* Howard shouted, getting in the spirit of the thing. His mother had taught him a few words of French. He held his little hands up for attention. *'Dix francs!'* A few more people stopped. American street-performers were a rarity.

Cybele shushed Howard. Jimmy started crying for an ice cream. Iris had one of the thorns and was practicing jabbing it into the aether. 'This is swell, Dad! Can I try it next?'

'We'll see, sweetie.' Raumer patted his daughter's blond head and kicked a raised foot tentatively. The thorn dug into the air. He reached up and set another thorn overhead. He was able then to pull himself up off the ground, resting on his anchored left foot and right hand.

He drew his right foot up a little higher than the other and kicked it in. Iris handed him the fourth thorn, and he set that up higher with his left hand. Like a human fly climbing an office building with suction cups, he began working his way up. A few coins rang on the pavement beneath him. *'Dix francs!'* Howard shouted again.

Cybele had just gotten four ice cream sticks from a vendor. Now she saw him and stared up, fear and joy fighting for possession of her features. 'Don't go too *high*, Charlie!'

He did another few meters. He was high enough to break a leg now if he fell. His hands were sweating and it was hard to keep a good grip on the thorns in his hands. The shafts of the other thorns were digging into the soles of his feet. He couldn't go much higher. But he didn't want to go back down to his family either.

The most puzzling thing was that the aether didn't seem to be moving relative to normal space. Using the sliding-coins analogy, a person would be a small, irregular coin riding the rim of a huge rotating disk . . . Earth. But since Earth is rotating, then it should zip out from under any piton fixed in the motionless aether. Of course maybe the aether wasn't quite solid after all. Maybe a thin sheet of it was dragged along with the Earth. Given the right kinds of length contractions that would just about jibe with relativity. Raumer wondered if he could set a thorn hard enough to reach the lower levels of the aether.

Holding fast with his left hand, he pulled his right hand back and slammed the thorn forward as hard as he could. There was a sudden wrench, the sound of glass breaking. His right hand was bleeding. The thorn had ripped out of his grasp and sped across the plaza to break a window in the Pompidou Center.

There were a lot of people under Raumer now, pointing at him and at the broken window. He was ten or fifteen meters up. Cybele and the kids seemed peculiarly unconcerned about him. They were just eating their ice creams and staring. Howard and Iris had managed to fill their pockets with small change from the crowd. Across the plaza Raumer saw a *flic*, a young nattily-uniformed policeman. He was heading his way. Raumer wondered how that African kid had managed to disappear.

He was standing on two of the thorns and holding the other with both hands. Now the *flic* was close enough to start shouting at him. Calling him a terrorist. He was going to have to do something. Before, it had looked as if that kid had just jumped backward . . . out through hyperspace. He'd done it himself that morning. But what if he landed wrong? Suddenly he didn't care.

Raumer tensed all his muscles and jumped backwards, pushing off as hard as possible with the three thorns. He slipped sideways as he took off.

And a sort of wafer floated to the ground

'*Qu'est-ce qu'il y a, alors?*' the *flic* asked, effortlessly pushing his way through the crowd. His handsome dark eyes flashed back and forth, searching for the man who had broken the window. But the villian had escaped.

In the center of the circle the *flic* found only a sidewalk artist . . . a charming French-American woman with three children. They were standing around an astonishingly detailed cross-sectional picture of a man's insides.

Strictly speaking, the *flic* should have arrested the woman for painting without a license. But suddenly, inexplicably, the picture seemed to slide off down the street. The policeman covered his confusion by asking the woman for a date.

The following selected passages, and the accompanying illustrations, are taken from TRANSDIMENSIONAL AVATAR by Revell Gibson (Ten Pound Island Press, 1982).

And how did this living avatar come into being? How is it that, Christ-like, one man can span the gap between Heaven and Hell . . . yet remain here on Earth with ordinary mortals?

Professor Raumer has suggested that I explain his physical transmogrification by the time-honored technique of analogical reasoning. So let us imagine a flat universe, a two-dimensional world whose inhabitants would contemplate the idea of a *third* dimension with the fear and trembling we normally accord the *fourth*.

We are three-dimensional solids that move about on a certain surface, the spherical surface of Earth. Think of a Flatland whose inhabitants are two-dimensional figures that move about on a certain line, the bounding line, if you will, or a disk which they call their planet.

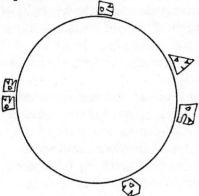

Just as gravity limits us, as a rule, to two degrees of freedom in our mundane peregrinations (East-West plus North-South); just so we imagine that the Flatland gravity limits most Flatlanders to one degree of freedom in their motions (Left-Right) along their planetary line. Of course, if a Flatlander had wing-like projections which he *flapped*, then

he could also move in the additional Up-Down dimension, just as a bird does.

Now suppose that the whole sheet which makes up Flatland is actually lying *on* something. Think of a vast sheet of wax paper floating on a sea. In the sheet itself are scratches . . . shapes which move about . . . the Flatlanders bustling back and forth on their planetary line. The analogy, of course, is to our space as a vast hypersheet nestled on the breast of the endless Aether main.

And what a noble vista that must be, the endless sea of Aethery! What strange demons swim beneath, what angels fly above! Our thoughts, Professor Raumer tells me, float above this sea like joyous, sun-bathed clouds . . . but *beneath* the hypersurface crowd clotted emotions: shining, stinging, slimy jellyfish!

Our avatar, our Professor Raumer, is wedged at right angles to our space. He is half above the hypersurface of space . . . and half below. Half-demon and half-god, he intersects our space in a single two-dimensional cross-section . . . a section too thin and feeble for speech, but immanent enough for hand-signals.

It fell upon me to be the first to recognize him for what he is, though so seemingly like a beer-stain on the floor . . . the floor of the Coupole Café to be precise, in the Montparnasse district of Paris. A marvelous place, crowded with merrymakers late into the night. I was there, part of the happy throng, eating my second dozen of oysters. *Claires No. 1* (the best in my estimation) were the oysters, and I gave this living food an agreeable environment in the form of a bottle of excellent, but cheap, Muscadet.

Full of food, full of peace, I gazed with interest at the floor. There were cigarette butts, women's ankles, streaks of sawdust and!!! A large, man-shaped stain, lightly tinted, a perfect silhouette sliding along! The arms were waving in semaphore, I realized proximately, still remembering my youthful experience as a signalman. 'H-E-L-P!' they said.

Without wishing to attract undue notice, I moved my feet about on the floor, also in semaphore patterns. 'W-H-O A-R-E Y-O-U?' An animated conversation ensued. Raumer had been sliding all over Paris looking for someone who would a) notice him, and b) understand his arm signals. I was, or am, the man, and will be, yet even in the face of scorn from those myopic fools who say they cannot *see* Professor Raumer.

But I digress. Professor Raumer's rotation was, he told me, the result of an ill-conceived and badly executed attempt to move out along the Aether, above the surface of the Earth, and against the gravitational force.

His technique was to use special thorns as *Oars* or *Pitons*, reaching out of our space and into the Aether, thus exerting a force to act against gravity. This worked well enough, but when he attempted to jump free of the Aether and back to the ground, he slipped somehow sideways.

Gravity, weakly acting on that of his cross-sections still in our space, keeps him glued to the ground. He floats, as it were, on his back. By sticking a leg or an arm down into the swirling currents of the Aether sea he is able to slide about Earth's surface at will. Yet, such is the nature of the Aetherstuff that Professor Raumer is unable to exert the force to turn himself sideways. His own efforts cannot bring him fully back into our space.

Immediately after the transformation, Professor Raumer slid away from the crowd at the Pompidou Center. He tells me that he was by some higher vision certain that his wife, a practical woman, would take up with the first replacement for him which she found. He could not have been more prescient.

These inquiries finally led me to an apartment above a miserable café in the Monceau district. Professor Raumer had so manipulated himself that only a cross-section of his head and eyes remained in our space. I carried this cross-section tucked between the pages of these very notes.

Throned behind the zinc bar was the inevitable *concierge*, a termagant, a virago. No, she had never heard of a Madame Raumer. I gave her twenty francs. Oh yes, I must be looking for the woman with the American children. She lived upstairs with her fiancé, a fine young man employed by the police force.

'*That*'s not my husband,' cried Mrs. Raumer, an attractive but somewhat hard-looking woman. 'My husband is *dead!*'

The cross-section of Professor Raumer's head lay on the table between us. Suddenly the shapes of his two hands appeared on the table-top as well. The fingers moved in agile silhouettes, spelling out the words of his plea: 'C-Y-B-E-L-E I S-T-I-L-L L-O-V-E Y-O-U. D-O Y-O-U H-A-V-E T-H-E T-H-O-R-N-S?'

Mrs. Raumer started back from the table. She seemed angry with me. 'Get out of here, you pompous *blimp!* Take your creepy *magic* tricks with you! No, I don't have the thorns, the thorns disappeared with my *husband!* He's *gone* and I have a new life!'

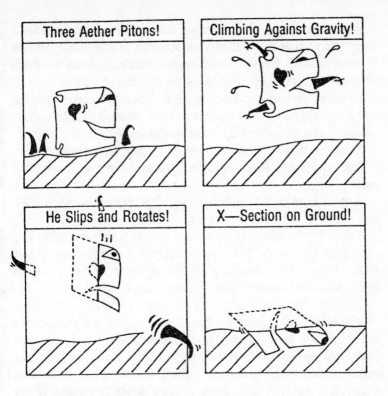

As she railed in this wise, one of her children, the littlest, pressed forward and poked a finger into the center of the cross-section on the table. This direct palpating of his brain must have been uncomfortable for Professor Raumer, for he slid off the table, floated to the floor, and disappeared beneath a rug.

The unpleasantly handsome young *flic* seemed to take me for his rival in Mrs. Raumer's affections. If I were not a man of generous bulk, the situation might have gone very badly indeed. As it was, I was forced to leave so precipitously that I was unable to retrieve Professor Raumer from beneath the rug. There was nothing for it but to install myself in the dreary drink-shop downstairs and await further developments.

I spent a miserable two hours there, with only a few pinball players for company. The café's menu was utterly without interest, and their wine was not even deplorable. I regretted having aided Professor Raumer in his fool's mission of revisiting his family. I had helped him only because of his promise to later reveal certain higher truths to me.

I was on the point of leaving when Raumer's three children suddenly appeared, trooping down the stairs. Iris, the oldest, was spokeswoman for this pathetic delegation.

'Can you make my Daddy get fat again?' she inquired.

'Perhaps I can help. But not unless he comes away with me.'

'I want him to stay under the rug,' protested Howard. 'We can talk to him with our fingers.'

Talk? About what? How absurd to waste so great an avatar on children's prattle! I controlled myself with difficulty. 'Your father belongs to humanity. With my help he can bring us unheard-of knowledge. Tell him he must come to me.'

It was almost midnight, and I was quite dizzy from the many glasses of cognac. The children had long since gone back upstairs. Bleakly I wondered how Professor Raumer could prefer their uncultured company to mine. Just then I saw the familiar stain come sliding down the stairs like a hesitant man's shadow.

The scene was painful in the extreme. Not having a family, and not wanting one, I cannot pretend to understand his motives. But in the end I promised to help him 'get fat again,' and for his part, Professor Raumer shared with me all that he had learned. I give here only a partial summary of what he told me that night before our long journey began.

Thoughts are definite forms . . . permanently extant, yet in some way parasitic upon human existence. *Parasitism* is too strong a word. Let us say, rather, *symbiosis*, reserving the term 'parasitism' for those low and slippery entities which do deserve such a name. I speak, of course, of human emotion, or, to be quite blunt, the ties of love which can make an avatar shrink from his destiny.

Following this, Professor Raumer described to me how the thought-clouds rain lower-dimensional simulacra of themselves upon the infinite Aether sea, dimpling and rippling the sketchy forms of our lowly three-dimensional space.

He told me of how the clouds merge and split, and of the great SUN beyond it all, the SUN which drives the eternal process of sublimation and precipitation. The SUN, the goal of every mystic's quest . . . I cannot understand how anyone could ever wish to leave it.

And now, these few notes written, we set off, I know not whence, in search of the sacred bush of *Shanker Bola*. With its thorns I will lever Professor Raumer back. With the same thorns I shall set myself free. Peace, my brothers.

CONVERSATION, AD 33

Arthur Schopenhauer

A: Have you heard the latest?
B: No, what's happened?
A: The world has been redeemed!
B: You don't say!
A: Yes, the Dear Lord took on human form and had himself executed in Jerusalem; and with that the world has been redeemed and the devil hoodwinked.
B: Gosh, that's simply lovely.

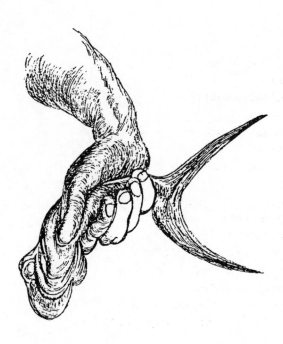

ANXIETY PLAY

Kurt Schwitters

a. Sir.
b. Yes?
a. You are under arrest.
b. No.
a. You are under arrest, Sir.
b. No.
a. I shall shoot, Sir.
b. No:
a. I shall shoot, Sir.
b. No.
a. I shall shoot, Sir.
b. No.
a. I hate you.
b. No.
a. I shall crucify you.
b. Not so.
a. I shall poison you.
b. Not so.
a. I shall murder you.
b. Not so.
a. Think of the winter.
b. Never.
a. I am going to kill you.
b. As I said, never.
a. I shall shoot.
b. You have already said that once.
a. Now come along.
b. You can't arrest me.
a. Why not?
b. You can take me into custody, but no more.

a. Then I shall take you into custody.
b. By all means.
    b. allows himself to be taken into custody and led away. The stage grows dark. The audience feels duped and there are catcalls and whistles. The chorus cries:
'Where's the author? Throw him out! Rubbish!'

ELEPHANT WITH WOODEN LEG

John Sladek

NOTE: MADMEN are often unable to distinguish between dream, reality, and . . . between dream and reality. None of the incidents in Henry LaFarge's narrative ever happened or could have happened. His 'Orinoco Institute' bears no relation to the actual think tank of that name, his 'Drew Blenheim' in no way resembles the famous futurologist, and his 'United States of America' is not even a burlesque upon the real United States of Armorica.

I couldn't hear him.

'Can't hear you, Blenheim. The line must be bad.'

'Or mad, Hank. I wonder what that would take?'

'What what?'

'What would it take to drive a telephone system out of its mind, eh? So that it wasn't just giving wrong numbers, but madly right ones. Let's see: Content-addressable computer memories to shift the conversations . . .'

I stopped listening. A bug was crawling up the window frame across the room. It moved like a cockroach, but I couldn't be sure.

'Look, Blenheim, I'm pretty busy today. Is there something on your mind?'

He ploughed right on. '. . . so if you're trying to reserve a seat on the plane to Seville, you'd get a seat at the opera instead. While the person who wants the opera seat is really making an appointment with a barber, whose customer is just then talking to the box-office of *Hair*, or maybe making a hairline reservation . . .'

'Blenheim, I'm talking to you.'

'Yes?'

'What was it you called me up about?'

'Oh, this and that. I was wondering, for instance, whether parrots have internal clocks.'

'What?' I still couldn't be sure whether the bug was a cockroach or not, but I saluted just in case.

'If so, maybe we could get them to act as speaking clocks.'

He sounded crazier than ever. What trivial projects for one of the best brains in our century – no wonder he was on leave.

'Blenheim, I'm busy. Institute work must go on, you know.'

'Yes. Tell you what, why don't you drop over this afternoon? I have something to talk over with you.'

'Can't. I have a meeting all afternoon.'

'Fine, fine. See you, then. Anytime around 4:43.'

Madmen never listen.

Helmut Rasmussen came in just as Blenheim hung up. He seemed distressed. Not that his face showed it; ever since that bomb wrecked his office, Hel has been unable to move his face. Hysterical paralysis, Dr. Grobe had explained.

But Hel could signal whatever he felt by fiddling with the stuff in his shirt pocket. For anger, his red pencil came out (and sometimes underwent a savage sharpening), impatience made him work his slide rule, surprise made him glance into his pocket diary, and so on.

Just now he was clicking the button on his ballpoint pen with some agitation. For a moment he actually seemed about to take it out and draw worry lines on his forehead.

'What is it, Hel? The costing on Project Faith?' He spread the schedules on my desk and pointed to the snag: a discrepancy between the estimated cost of blasting apart and hauling away the Rocky Mountains, and the value of oil recovered in the process.

'I see. The trains, eh? Diesels seem to use most of the oil we get. How about steam locomotives, then?'

He clapped me on the shoulder and nodded.

'By the way, Hel, I won't be at the meeting today. Blenheim just called up. Wants to see me.'

Hel indicated surprise.

'Look, I know he's a crackpot. You don't have to pocket-diary me, I know he's nuts. But he is also technically still the Director. Our boss. They haven't taken him off the payroll, just put him on sick leave. Besides, he used to have a lot of good ideas.'

Hel took out a felt-tip pen and began to doodle with some sarcasm. The fact was, Blenheim had completely lost his grip during his last year at the Institute. Before the government forced him to take leave, he'd been spending half a million a year on developing, rumours said, glass pancakes. And who could forget his plan to arm police with chocolate revolvers?

'Sure he's had a bad time, but maybe he's better now,' I said, without conviction.

Institute people never get better, Hel seemed to retort. They just kept on making bigger and better decisions, with more and more brilliance and finality, until they broke. Like glass pancakes giving out an ever purer ring, they exploded.

It was true. Like everyone else here, I was seeing Dr. Grobe, our resident psychiatrist, several times a week. Then there were cases beyond even the skill of Dr. Grobe: Joe Feeney, who interrupted his work (on the uses of holograms) one day to announce that he was a filing cabinet. Edna Bessler, who believed that she was being pursued by a synthetic *a priori* proposition. The lovely entomologist Pawlie Sutton, who disappeared. And George Hoad, whose rocket research terminated when he walked into the Gents one day and cut his throat. George spent the last few minutes of consciousness vainly trying to mop up the bloody floor with toilet paper . . .

Something was wrong with the personnel around this place, all right. And I suspected that our little six-legged masters knew more about this than they were saying.

Finally I mumbled, 'I know it's useless, Hel. But I'd better find out what he wants.'

You do what you think is best, Hel thought. He stalked out of my office then, examining the point on his red pencil.

The bug was a cockroach, *P. americana*. It sauntered across the wall until it reached the curly edge of a wall poster, then it flew about a foot to land on the nearest dark spot. This was Uncle Sam's right eye. Uncle Sam, with his accusing eyes and finger, was trying to recruit men for the Senate and House of Representatives. On this poster, he said, 'The Senate Needs MEN'. So far, the recruitment campaign was a failure. Who could blame people for not wanting to go on the 'firing line' in Washington? The casualty rate of Congressmen was 30 per cent annually, and climbing, in spite of every security measure we could think of.

Which reminded me of work. I scrubbed off the blackboard and started laying out a contingency tree for Project Pogo, a plan to make the whole cabinet – all one hundred and forty-three secretaries – completely mobile, hence, proof against revolution. So far the Security Secretary didn't care for the idea of 'taking to our heels', but it was cheaper to keep the cabinet on the move than to guard them in Washington.

The cockroach, observing my industry, left by a wall ventilator, and I breathed easier. The contingency tree didn't look so interesting by now, and out the window I could see real trees.

The lawn rolled away down from the building to the river (not the Orinoco, despite our name). The far bank was blue-black with pines, and the three red maples on our lawn, this time of year, stood out like three separate, brilliant fireballs. For just the duration of a bluejay's flight from one to another, I could forget about the stale routine, the smell of chalkdust.

I remembered a silly day three years ago, when I'd carved a heart on one of those trees, with Pawlie Sutton's initials and my own.

Now a security guard strolled his puma into view. They stopped under the nearest maple and he snapped the animal's lead. It was up the trunk in two bounds, and out of sight among the leaves. While that stupid-faced man in uniform looked up, the fireball shook and swayed above him. A few great leaves fell, bright as drops of blood.

Now what was *this* headache going to be about?

All the big problems were solved, or at least we knew how to solve them. The world was just about the way we wanted it, now, except we no longer seemed to want it that way. That's how Mr. Howell, the Secretary of Personal Relationships, had put it in his telecast. What was missing? God, I think he said. God had made it possible for us to dam the Amazon and move the Orinoco, to feed India and dig gold from the ocean floor and cure cancer. And now God – the way he said it made you feel that He, too, was in the Cabinet – God was going to help us get down and solve our personal, human problems. Man's inhumanity to man. The lack of communication. The hatred. God and Secretary Howell were going to get right down to some committee work on this. I think that was the telecast where Howell announced the introduction of detention camps for 'malcontents'. Just until we got our personal problems all ironed out. I had drawn up the plans for these camps that summer. Then George Hoad borrowed my pocket-knife one day and never gave it back. Then the headaches started.

As I stepped outside, the stupid-faced guard was looking up the skirt of another tree.

'Prrt, prrt,' he said quietly, and the black puma dropped to earth beside him. There was something hanging out of its mouth that looked like a bluejay's wing.

'Good girl. Good girl.'

I hurried away to the helicopter.

Drew Blenheim's tumbledown mansion sits in the middle of withered woods. For half a mile around, the trees are laced together with high-voltage fence. Visitors are blindfolded and brought in by helicopter. There are also rumours of minefields and other security measures. At that time, I put it all down to Blenheim's paranoia.

The engine shut down with the sound of a coin spinning to rest. Hands helped me out and removed my blindfold. The first thing I saw, hanging on a nearby stretch of fence, was a lump of bones and burnt fur from some small animal. The guards and their submachine-guns escorted me only as far as the door, for Blenheim evidently hated seeing signs of the security he craved. The house looked dismal and decayed – the skull of some dead Orinoco Institute?

A servant wearing burnt cork makeup and white gloves ushered me through a dim hallway that smelled of hay and on into the library.

'I'll tell Mr. Blenheim you're here, sir. Perhaps you'd care to read one of his monographs while you wait?'

I flicked through *The Garden of Regularity* (a slight tract recommending that older people preserve intestinal health by devouring their own dentures) and opened an insanely boring book called *Can Bacteria Read?* I was staring uncomprehendingly at one of its pages when a voice said:

'Are you still here?' The plump old woman had evidently been sitting in her deep chair when I came in. As she craned around at me, I saw she had a black eye. Something was wrong with her hair, too. 'I thought you'd left by now – oh, it's *you*.'

'Madam, do I know you?'

She sat forward and put her face to the light. The black eye was tattooed, and the marcelled hair was really a cap of paper, covered with wavy ink lines. But it was Edna Bessler, terribly aged.

'You've changed, Edna.'

'So would you, young man, if you'd been chased around a nuthouse for two years by a synthetic *a priori* proposition.' She sniffed. 'Well, thank heavens the revolution is set for tomorrow.'

I laughed nervously. 'Well, Edna, it certainly is good to see you. What are you doing here, anyway?'

'There are quite a few of the old gang here, Joe Feeney and – and others. This place has become a kind of repair depot for mad futurologists. Blenheim is very kind, but of course he's quite mad himself. Mad as a wet hen. As you see from his writing.'

'*Can Bacteria Read?* I couldn't read it.'

'Oh, he thinks that germs are, like people, amenable to suggestion. So, with the proper application of mass hypnosis among the microbe populations, we ought to be able to cure any illness with any quack remedy.'

I nodded. 'Hope he recovers soon. I'd like to see him back at the Institute, working on real projects again. Big stuff, like the old days. I'll never forget the old Drew Blenheim, the man who invented satellite dialling.'

Satellite dialling came about when the malcontents were trying to jam government communications systems, cut lines and blow up exchanges. Blenheim's system virtually made each telephone a complete exchange in itself, dialling directly through a satellite. Voice signals were compressed and burped skywards in short bursts that evaded most jamming signals. It was an Orinoco Institute triumph over anarchy.

Edna chuckled. 'Oh, he's working on real projects. I said he was mad, not useless. Now if you'll help me out of this chair, I must go fix an elephant.'

I was sure I'd misheard this last. After she'd gone, I looked over a curious apparatus in the corner. Parts of it were recognizable – a clock inside a parrot cage, a gas laser, and a fringed shawl suspended like a flag from a walking-stick thrust into a watermelon – but their combination was baffling.

At 4:43 by the clock in the cage, the blackface servant took me to a gloomy great hall place, scattered with the shapes of easy chairs and sofas. A figure in a diving suit rose from the piano and waved me to a chair. Then it sat down again, flipping out its airhoses behind the bench.

For a few minutes I suffered through a fumbling version of some Mexican tune. But when Blenheim – no doubt it was he

– stood up and started juggling oranges, I felt it was time to speak out.

'Look, I've interrupted my work to come here. Is this all you have to show me?'

One of the oranges vaulted high, out of sight in the gloom above; another hit me in the chest. The figure opened its face-plate and grinned. 'Long time no see, Hank.'

It was me.

'Rubber mask,' Blenheim explained, plucking at it. 'I couldn't resist trying it on you, life gets so tedious here. Ring for Rastus, will you? I want to shed this suit.'

We made small talk while the servant helped him out of the heavy diving suit. Rather, Blenheim rattled on alone; I wasn't feeling well at all. The shock of seeing myself had reminded me of something I should remember, but couldn't.

'. . . to build a heraldry vending machine. Put in a coin, punch out your name, and it prints a coat-of-arms. Should suit those malcontents, eh? All they probably really want is a coat-of-arms.'

'They're just plain evil,' I said. 'When I think how they bombed poor Hel Rasmussen's office –'

'Oh, he did that himself. Didn't you know?'

'Suicide? So that explains the hysterical paralysis!'

My face looked exasperated, as Blenheim peeled it off. 'Is that what Dr. Grobe told you? Paralysed hell, the blast blew his face clean off. Poor Hel's present face is a solid plate of plastic, bolted on. He breathes through a hole in his shoulder and feeds himself at the armpit. If Grobe told you any different, he's just working on your morale.'

From upstairs came a kind of machine-gun clatter. The minstrel servant glided in with a tray of drinks.

'Oh, Rastus. Tell the twins not to practise their tap-dancing just now, will you? Hank looks as if he has a headache.'

'Yes sir. By the way, the three-legged elephant has arrived.

I put it in the front hall. I'm afraid the prosthesis doesn't fit.'

'I'll fix it. Just ask Jumbo to lean up against the wall for half an hour.'

'Very good, sir.'

After this, I decided to make my escape from this Bedlam. 'Doesn't anybody around here ever do anything straight-forward or say anything in plain English?'

'We're trying to tell you something, Hank, but it isn't easy. For one thing, I'm not sure we can trust you.'

'Trust me for what?'

His twisted face twisted out a smile. 'If you don't know, then how can we trust you? But come with me to the conservatory and I'll show you something.'

We went to a large room with dirty glass walls. To me it looked like nothing so much as a bombed-out workshop. Though there were bags of fertilizer on the floor, there wasn't a living plant in sight. Instead, the tables were littered with machinery and lab equipment: jumbles of retorts and coloured wires and nuts and bolts that made no sense.

'What do you see, Hank?'

'Madness and chaos. You might as well have pears in the light sockets and a banana on the telephone cradle, for all I can make of it.'

He laughed. 'That's better. We'll crazify you yet.'

I pointed to a poster-covered cylinder standing in the corner. One of the posters had Uncle Sam, saying 'I Need MEN for Congress'.

'What's that Parisian advertising kiosk doing here?'

'Rastus built that for us, out of scrap alloys I had lying around. Like it?'

I shrugged. 'The top's too pointed. It looks like –'

'Yes, go on.'

'This is silly. All of you need a few sessions with Dr. Grobe,' I said. 'I'm leaving.'

'I was afraid you'd say that. But it's you who need another

235

session with Dr. Grobe, Hank.'

'You think *I'm* crazy?'

'No, you're too damned sane.'

'Well you sure as hell are nuts!' I shouted. 'Why bother with all the security outside? Afraid someone will steal the idea of a minstrel show or the secret of a kiosk?'

He laughed again. 'Hank, those guards aren't there to keep strangers out. *They're to keep us in.* You see, my house really and truly is a madhouse.'

I stamped out a side door and ordered my helicopter.

'My head's killing me,' I told the guard. 'Take it easy with that blindfold.'

'Oh, sorry, mac. Hey look, it's none of my business, but what did you do with that tree you brung with you?'

'Tree?' God, even the guards were catching it.

That evening I went to see Dr. Grobe.

'Another patient? I swear, I'm going to install a revolving door on this office. Sit down. Uh, Hank LaFarge, isn't it? Sit down, Hank. Let's see . . . oh, you're the guy who's afraid of cockroaches, right?'

'Not exactly afraid of them. In fact they remind me of someone I used to be fond of. Pawlie Sutton used to work with them. But my problem is, I know that cockroaches are the real bosses. We're just kidding ourselves with our puppet government, our Uncle Sham –'

He chuckled appreciatively.

'But what "bugs" me is, nobody will recognize this plain and simple truth, Doctor.'

'Ah, ah. Remember last time, you agreed to call me by my first name.'

'Sorry, uh, Oddpork.' I couldn't imagine why anyone with that name wanted to be called by it, unless the doctor himself was trying to get used to it. He was an odd-pork of a man, too: plump and rumpy, with over-large hands that never stopped adjusting his already well-adjusted clothes. He always looked surprised at everything I said, even 'hello'. Every session, he made the same joke about the revolving door.

Still, repetitive jokes help build a family atmosphere, which was probably what he wanted. There was a certain comfort in this stale atmosphere of no surprises. Happy families are all alike, and their past is exactly like their future.

'Hank, I haven't asked you directly about your cockroach theory before, have I? Want to tell me about it?'

'I know it sounds crazy at first. For one thing, cockroaches aren't very smart, I know that. In some ways, they're stupider than ants. And their communication equipment isn't much, either. Touch and smell, mainly. They aren't naturally equipped for conquering the world.'

Oddpork lit a cigar and leaned back, looking at the ceiling. 'What do they do with the world when they get it?'

'That's another problem. After all, they don't *need* the world. All they need is food, water, a fair amount of darkness and some warmth. But there's the key, you see?

'I mean we humans have provided for all these needs for many centuries. Haphazardly, though. So it stands to reason that life would be better for them if we worked for them on a regular basis. But to get us to do that, they have to take over first.'

He tried to blow a smoke ring, failed, and adjusted his tie. 'Go on. How do they manage this takeover?'

'I'm not sure, but I think they have help. Maybe some smart tinkerer wanted to see what would happen if he gave them good long-distance vision. Maybe he was so pleased with the result that he then taught them to make semaphore signals with their feelers. The rest is history.'

Dusting his lapel, Dr. Grobe said, 'I don't quite follow. Semaphore signals?'

'One cockroach is stupid. But a few thousand of them in good communication could make up a fair brain. Our tinkerer probably hastened that along by intensive breeding and group

237

learning problems, killing off the failures . . . it would take ten years at the outside.'

'Really? And how long would the conquest of man take? How would the little insects fare against the armies of the world?'

'They never need to try. Armies are run by governments, and governments are run, for all practical purposes, by small panels of experts. Think tanks like the Orinoco Institute. And – this just occurred to me – for all practical purposes, you run the Institute.'

For once, Dr. Grobe did not looked surprised. 'Oh, so I'm in on the plot, am I?'

'We're all so crazy, we really depend on you. You can ensure that we work for the good of the cockroaches, or else you can get rid of us – send us away, or encourage our suicides.'

'Why should I do that?'

'Because *you* are afraid of them.'

'Not at all.' But his hand twitched, and a little cigar ash fell on his immaculate trousers. I felt my point was proved.

'Damn. I'll have to sponge that. Excuse me.'

He stepped into his private washroom and closed the door. My feeling of triumph suddenly faded. Maybe I was finally cracking. What evidence did I really have?

On the other hand, Dr. Grobe was taking a long time in there. I stole over to the washroom door and listened.

'. . . verge of suicide . . .,' he murmured. '. . . yes . . . give up the idea, but . . . yes, that's just what I . . .'

I threw back the door on a traditional spy scene. In the half-darkness, Dr. G was hunched over the medicine cabinet, speaking into a microphone. He wore earphones.

'Hank, don't be a foo –'

I hit him, not hard, and he sat down on the edge of the tub. He looked resigned.

'So this is my imagined conspiracy, is it? Where do these wires lead?'

They led inside the medicine cabinet, to a tiny apparatus.

A dozen brown ellipses had clustered around it, like a family around the TV.

'Let me explain,' he said.

'Explanations are unnecessary, Doctor. I just want to get out of here, unless your six-legged friends can stop me.'

'They might. So could I. I could order the guards to shoot you. I could have you put away with your crazy friends. I could even have you tried for murder, just now.'

'Murder?' I followed his gaze back into the office. From under the desk, a pair of feet. 'Who's that?'

'Hel Rasmussen. Poisoned himself a few minutes before you came in. Believe me, it wasn't pleasant, seeing the poor fellow holding a bottle of cyanide to his armpit. He left a note blaming you, in a way.'

'Me!'

'You were the last straw. This afternoon, he saw you take an axe and deliberately cut down one of those beautiful maple trees in the yard. Destruction of beauty – it was too much for him.'

Trees again. I went to the office window and looked out at the floodlit landscape. One of the maples was missing.

Dr. Grobe and I sat down again at our respective interview stations, while I thought this over. Blenheim and his mask came into it, I was sure of that. But why?

Dr. Grobe fished his lifeless cigar from the ashtray. 'The point is, I can stop you from making any trouble for me. So you may as well hear me out.' He scratched a match on the sole of Hel's shoe and relit the cigar.

'All right, Oddpork. You win. What happens now?'

'Nothing much. Nothing at all. If my profession has any meaning, it's to keep things from happening.' He blew out the match. 'I'm selling ordinary life. Happiness, as you must now see, lies in developing a pleasant, comfortable and productive routine – and then sticking to it. No unpleasant surprises. No

239

shocks. Psychiatry has always aimed for that, and now it is within our grasp. The cockroach conspiracy hasn't taken over the world, but it has taken over the Institute – and it's our salvation.

'You see, Hank, our bargain isn't one-sided. We give them a little shelter, a few scraps of food. But they give us something far more important: real organization. *The life of pure routine.*'

I snorted. 'Like hurrying after trains? Or wearing ourselves out on assembly-line work? Or maybe grinding our lives away in boring offices? Punching time-clocks and marching in formation?'

'None of the above, thank you. Cockroaches never hurry to anything but dinner. They wouldn't march in formation except for fun. They are free – yet they are part of a highly organized society. And this can be ours.'

'If we're not all put in detention camps.'

'Listen, those camps are only a stage. So what if a few million grumblers get sterilized and shut away for a year or two? Think of the *billions* of happy, decent citizens, enjoying a freedom they have earned. Someday, every man will live exactly as he pleases – and his pleasure will lie in serving his fellow men.'

Put like that, it was persuasive. Another half-hour of this and I was all but convinced.

'Sleep on it, eh Hank? Let me know tomorrow what you think.' His large hand on my shoulder guided me to the door.

'You may be right,' I said, smiling back at him. I meant it, too. Even though the last thing I saw, as the door closed, was a stream of glistening brown that came from under the washroom door and disappeared under the desk.

I sat up in my own office most of the night, staring out at the maple stump. There was no way out: Either I worked for *Periplaneta americana* and gradually turned into a kind of moral cockroach myself, or I was killed. And there were certain advantages to either choice.

I was about to turn on the video-recorder to leave a suicide note, when I noticed the cassette was already recorded. I ran it back and played it.

Blenheim came on, wearing my face and my usual suit.

'They think I'm you, Hank, dictating some notes. Right now you're really at my house, reading a dull book in the library. So dull, in fact, that it's guaranteed to put you into a light trance. When I'm safely back, Edna will come in and wake you.

'She's not as loony as she seems. The black eye is inked for her telescope, and the funny cap with lines on it, that looks like marcelled hair, that's a weathermap. I won't explain why she's doing astronomy – you'll understand in time.

'On the other hand, she's got a fixation that the stars are nothing but the shiny backs of cockroaches, treading around the heavenly spheres. It makes a kind of sense when you think of it: *Periplaneta* means around the world, and America being the home of the Star-Spangled Banner.

'Speaking of national anthems, Mexico's is La Cucaracha – another cockroach reference. They seem to be taking over this message!

'The gang and I have been thinking about bugs a lot lately. Of course Pawlie has always thought about them, but the rest of us . . .' I missed the next part. So Pawlie was at the madhouse? And they hadn't told me?

'. . . when I started work on the famous glass pancakes. I discovered a peculiar feature of glass discs, such as those found on clock faces.

'Say, you can do us a favour. I'm coming around at dawn with the gang, to show you a gadget or two. We haven't got all the bugs out of them yet, but – will you go into Dr. Grobe's office at dawn, and check the time on his clock? But first, smash the glass on his window, will you? Thanks. I'll compensate him for it later.

'Then go outside the building, but on no account stand between the maple stump and the broken window. The best place to wait is on the little bluff to the North, where you'll have a good view of the demonstration. We'll meet you there.

'Right now you see our ideas darkly, as through a pancake, I guess. But soon you'll understand. You see, we're a kind of cockroach ourselves. I mean, living on scraps of sanity. We have to speak in parables and work in silly ways because *they* can't. *They* live in a comfortable kind of world where elephants have their feet cut off to make umbrella stands. We have to make good use of the three-legged elephants.

'Don't bother destroying this cassette. It won't mean a thing to any right-living insect.'

It didn't mean much to me, not yet. Cockroaches in the stars? Clocks? There were questions I had to ask, at the rendezvous.

There was one question I'd already asked that needed an answer. Pawlie had been messing about in her lab, when I asked her to marry me. Two years ago, was it? Or three?

'But you don't like cockroaches,' she said.

'No, and I'll never ask a cockroach for its claw in marriage.' I looked over her shoulder into the glass case. 'What's so interesting about these?'

'Well, for one thing, they're not laboratory animals. I caught them myself in the basement here at the Institute. See? Those roundish ones are the nymphs – sexless adolescents. Cute, aren't they?'

I had to admit they were. A little. 'They look like the fat black exclamation points in comic strips,' I observed.

'They're certainly healthy, all of them. I've never seen any like them. I – that's funny.' She went and fetched a book, and looked from some illustration to the specimens under glass.

'What's funny?'

'Look, I'm going to be dissecting the rest of the afternoon. Meet you for dinner. Bye.'

'You haven't answered my question, Pawlie.'

'Bye.'

That was the last I saw of her. Later, Dr. Grobe put it about that she'd been found, hopelessly insane. Still later, George Hoad cut his throat.

The floodlights went off, and I could see dawn greyness

and mist. I took a can of beans and went for a stroll outside.

One of the guards nodded a wary greeting. They and their cats were always jumpiest at this time of day.

'Everything all right, officer?'

'Yeah. Call me crazy, but I think I just heard an elephant.'

When he and his puma were out of sight, I heaved the can of beans through Dr. Grobe's lighted window.

'What the hell?' he shouted. I slipped back to my office, waited a few minutes, then went to see him.

A slender ray came through the broken window and struck the clock on the opposite wall. Grobe sat transfixed, staring at it with more surprise than ever. And no wonder, for the clock had become a parrot.

'Relax, Oddpork,' I said. 'It's only some funny kind of hologram in the clock face, worked by a laser from the lawn. You look like a comic villain, sitting there with that cigar stub in your face.'

The cigar stub moved. Looking closer, I saw it was made up of the packed tails of a few cockroaches, trying to force themselves between his closed lips. More ran up from his spotless collar and joined them, and others made for his nostrils. One approached the queue at the mouth, found another stuck there, and had a nibble at its kicking hind leg.

'Get away! Get away!' I gave Grobe a shake to dislodge them, and his mouth fell open. A brown flood of kicking bodies tumbled out and down, over his well-cut lapels.

I had stopped shuddering by the time I joined the others on the bluff. Pawlie and Blenheim were missing. Edna stopped scanning the horizon with her brass telescope long enough to introduce me to the pretty twins, Alice and Celia. They sat in the grass beside a tangled heap of revolvers, polishing their patent-leather tap shoes.

The ubiquitous Rastus was wiping off his burnt cork makeup. I asked him why.

243

'Don't need it anymore. Last night it was my camouflage. I was out in the woods, cutting a path through the electric fence. Quite a wide path, as you'll understand.'

He continued removing the black until I recognized the late George Hoad.

'George! But you cut your throat, remember? Mopping up blood –'

'Hank, that was your blood. It was you cut your throat in the Gents, After Pawlie vanished. Remember?'

I did, giddily. 'What happened to you, then?'

'Your suicide attempt helped me make up my mind; I quit the Institute next day. You were still in the hospital.'

Still giddy, I turned to watch Joe Feeney operating the curious laser I'd seen in the library. Making parrots out of clocks.

'I understand now,' I said. 'But what's the watermelon for?'

'Cheap cooling device.'

'And the "flag"?' I indicated the shawl-stick arrangement.

'To rally round. I stuck it in the melon because they were using the umbrella stand for –'

'Look!' Edna cried. 'The attack begins!' She handed me a second telescope.

All I saw below was the lone figure of Blenheim in his diving suit, shuffling slowly up from the river mist to face seven guards and two pumas. He seemed to be juggling croquet balls.

'Why don't we help him?' I shouted. 'Don't just sit there shining shoes and idling.'

The twins giggled. 'We've already helped some,' said Alice, nodding at the pile of weapons. 'We made friends with the guards.'

I got the point when those below pulled their guns on Blenheim. As each man drew, he looked at his gun and then threw it away.

'What a waste,' Celia sighed. 'Those guns are made from just about the best chocolate you can get.'

Blenheim played his parlour trick on the nearest guard: one juggled ball flew high, the guard looked up, and a second ball clipped him on the upturned chin.

Now the puma guards went into action.

'I can't look,' I said, my eye glued to the telescope. One of the animals stopped to sniff at a sticky revolver, but the other headed straight for his quarry. He leapt up, trying to fasten his claws into the stranger's big brass head.

Out of the river mist came a terrible cry, and then a terrible sight: a hobbling grey hulk that resolved into a charging elephant. Charging diagonally, so it looked even larger.

The pumas left the scene. One fled in our direction until Alice snatched up a pistol and fired it in the air. At that sound, the guards decided to look for jobs elsewhere. After all, as Pawlie said later, you couldn't expect a man to face a juggling diver *and* a mad elephant with a wooden leg, with nothing but a chocolate .38, not on *those* wages.

Pawlie was riding on the neck of the elephant. When he came to a wobbling stop I saw that one of Jumbo's forelegs was a section of tree with the bark still on it. And in the bark, a heart with PS+HL, carved years before.

I felt the triumph was all over – especially since Pawlie kept nodding her head yes at me – until George said:

'Come on, gang. Let's set it up.'

Jumbo had been pulling a wooden sledge, bearing the Paris kiosk. Now he went off to break his fast on water and grass, while the rest of us set the thing upright. Even before we had fuelled it with whatever was in the fertilizer bags, I guessed that it was a rocket.

After some adjustments, the little door was let down, and a sweet, breakfast pancake odour came forth. Joe Feeney opened a flask of dark liquid and poured it in the entrance. The smell grew stronger.

'Maple sap,' he explained. 'From Jumbo's wooden leg. Mixed with honey. And there's oatmeal inside. A farewell breakfast.'

I looked in the little door and saw the inside of the ship was made like a metal honeycomb, plenty of climbing room for our masters.

Pawlie came from the building with a few cockroaches in a jar, and let them taste our wares. Then, all at once, it was a sale opening at any big department store. We all stood back and let the great brown wave surge forward and break over the little rocket. Some of them, nymphs especially, scurried all the way up to the nose cone and back down again in their excitement. It all looked so jolly that I tried not to think about their previous meals.

Edna glanced at her watch. 'Ten minutes more,' she said. 'Or they'll hit the sun.'

I objected that we'd never get all of them loaded in ten minutes.

'No,' said Pawlie, 'but we'll get the best and strongest. The shrews can keep the rest in control.'

Edna closed the door, and the twins did a vigorous tap-dance on the unfortunate stragglers. A few minutes later, a million members of the finest organization on earth were on their way to the stars.

'To join their little friends,' said Edna.

Pawlie and I touched hands, as Blenheim opened his faceplate.

'I've been making this study,' he said, 'of spontaneous combustion in giraffes . . .'

KEYNSHAM

Vivian Stanshall

IN THE dental-white district of Keynsham stands the Thermometer Zoo. The ferocious bushy-faced villagers of Keynsham hate the inmates of the Thermometer Zoo and as they go about their work, the wet sacks jingling on their humped chests, they glare angrily up at the grey-stone buildings high on the slopes of the Silver Mountain outside the walls. They dream of the day when they will draw the Leg from its scabbard and push it up the slopes of the Silver Mountain and break the walls of the grey-stone building. And then they will use their chests to buffet, and their teeth to bite, and their tongues to touch.

But inside the asylum it is cool and shiny with tiles and tubes and the sound of throats.

In Keynsham there is a great shouting near the gate. One of the dwarfs has caught a fox. It is the first time he has tasted flesh for many days because of the Smell. A crowd gathers to watch him poke the greasy segments through the curved lips of his mask.

It is the Festival of the Snail and there is a fair in the village. A stall sells 'muscular' oranges wrapped in tissue-thin rubber and a side-show exhibits an orchestra of deranged mortgagees and their families who stroke sad music from carved instruments of strange design. Two intelligent horses sewn in a man-suit are startled by the yelps of the crowd and burst from their costume in disjointed panic. Under the walls, in the alleys slippery with wipes, are erected rows of tents for the tattooists, leechers and masseurs. Outside the largest tent several revellers squat in silence, listening for the buzz and gasps from within. In this tent, by means of a new invention, a man is being decorated and experiencing the precise sensations of hanging. He emerges to a storm of applause, rolling down his sleeve and bowing self-consciously.

> 'Transmogrify,' the jackals speak,
> The worms are feeding on our cheeks;
> 'Transmute,' the time flies quickly past
> And Keynsham arms with lies and masks.

From Keynsham a hideous throng rushes out; fierce with feathers, masked and painted, reeking of waters; sheep-like on all fives. First the Berserks, scarred, gargantuan, drugged with roots: stamping and biting on their shields, feverish with hate. Next the contortionists, greased and expectant. Now come the Apostates with shaven heads and faces grey with asheesh, singing sweetly and complaining with censers of myrrh and towing huge wardrobes from which they choose new veils. (Singing and swinging in a rhesus proboscis way.) Between their skirts run the Dwarfs and Defecators and Dylantines endlessly quoting in the wake of the Vegetable Normopaths who sow the Earth with asterisks that the Children of If may harvest Boredom. The Amputees lining the route are excited and their truncated capers and squeals signify. . . . Most Glorious of All . . . the Coming of the Leg!

In the green forest the Watcher turns away and covers his face. He has seen the Leg and his vigil is over. The mental-pygmies screech from the branches: 'Stay? Stay?' . . . but he is gone! The Leg . . . O heavenly Vision. And astride it, shining like a toad . . . Norry Berg, sleek as raincoats, slippery as haddocks, saturnine and cruel. Bartering flesh in robes of richest skin.

And the crowd knelt before the God and some so far back, seeing nothing, so sickened by the squeeze and hot breath of the horde; blinded with percentages, numb with numbers and deafened by the clicking ciphers cried out. OUT. OUT!!! and he was . . . refreshed and caused to be drawn up an Equator of Greed. A contract to encompass the whole world, strangling several thousand unlucky Chinamen standing end to end and disappearing up his own accountant. And so on and so on, nearer and nearer in rhythmic progression and constant squirt-squirty. . . .

And it came to pass a great storm and ocean-going liners were flung about like matchboxes in the boiling ferment and the drained white bodies of drowned sailors made a soft blanket for the shores of the sea. And on the land, an earthquake of such dreadful effect that Graves cracked and said that Siegfried was really a shit. And the stink of the dead's gangrene hung in the atmosphere in a sweet pestilential cloud.

But the sky over Keynsham was clear and blue and filled with giant birds bristling with stars, and non-stick frying pans ringing and bashing like Ragnar's halls, and bootee-style brick shirts studded with ketchup and diamonds. But in the Museums deep in the catacombs where chains have teeth and priceless collections of silk socks shine in cabinets, ageing bestial courtesans injected themselves with paraffin and became so enormous that they clogged the tunnels. In the streets, the Dwarfs ran amok and spread fish-paste on the windows of tailors' shops and delicatessens. They seized the terrified Rhino as he snuffled near a roll-mop barrel and put a helmet of sardines on his head. They stuck a gherkin on his nose and they beat him with whippy sticks and they made him wear a sign round his neck that read: 'HELLO, I AM PLANTIMAL. INSIST ON VAN SMEERENS'. On the walls the Rabbit showed forty-five films describing Don Quixote in seventeen positions in marble, celluloid and plaster bas-relief; lectured on the Symbolism of Trousers in Renaissance Thought, the Importance of F in Art and followed with a short quiz accompanying himself on the euphonium 'Working backwards thru' the Norm. Nora, No, No, NO. The 3 is magic. (Trinity.) Walking under ladders? Tut, tut, Jacob. Ascend! Rising early in the morning . . . monochrome Seurat Room (or Engine of the House). Room 1225 is merely Room 1335A but the number has been changed because the band don't know it. Proven by ordeal. A Trilogy affording a contemporary gander at the Flasher Idea. Conan on the Khyber? *Mais, oui, certainement.*

Does that answer your question?

Now read on. . . .

SOURCES AND ACKNOWLEDGEMENTS

'The Corpse Car' by Alphonse Allais, translated by Miles Kington, from *The World of Alphonse Allais* (Chatto & Windus, 1969), translation copyright ©1969 by Miles Kington. Reprinted by permission of Miles Kington and Pan Books.

'The Kugelmass Episode' by Woody Allen, from *Side Effects* (Random House, 1980), copyright ©1980 by Woody Allen. Reprinted by permission of Random House, Inc.

'The Disappearance of Honoré Subrac' by Guillaume Apollinaire, from *The Wandering Jew, and other stories*, translated by Rémy Inglis Hall (Rupert Hart-Davis, 1967), translation copyright ©1965 by Rémy Inglis Hall. Reprinted by permission of Sir Rupert Hart-Davis.

'Brain Damage' by Donald Barthelme, from *City Life* (Farrar, Straus, 1970), copyright ©1970 by Donald Barthelme. Reprinted by permission of Farrar, Straus & Giroux, Inc.

'How to Appear in a Good Light to a Woman Passing in the Street' by André Breton, from *Le Manifeste du Surréalisme* (1924), reprinted by permission of J.J. Pauvert.

'My Flannel Knickers' by Leonora Carrington, from *The Seventh Horse, and other stories* (Dutton, 1988), copyright ©1988 by Leonora Carrington. Reprinted by permission of E.P. Dutton, Inc.

'Unacceptable Mixture' by Leopoldo Chariarse reprinted by permission of Atlas Press.

'The Angry Street' by G.K. Chesterton, from *The Daily News*, 25 Jan., 1908 as 'A Somewhat Improbable Story'. Collected in *Tremendous Trifles* (Methuen, 1909).

'The Mannekin with the Sugar Nose' by Salvador Dali, from *The Secret Life of Salvador Dali* (Vision Press, 1961), copyright ©1942 by the Estate of Salvador Dali.

'Meet My Maker' by J.P. Donleavy, from *Meet My Maker The Mad Molecule* (Bodley Head, 1965), copyright ©1965 by J.P. Donleavy. Reprinted by permission of the Author and Random Century Group.

'The Key is Frank' by Bob Dylan, from sleeve-notes to *John Wesley Harding* (CBS, 1968) collected as 'Three Kings' in *Bob Dylan: Writings and Drawings* (Cape, 1973), copyright ©1968 by Bob Dylan. Reprinted by permission of the Author's Agents.

'The Passion Considered as an Uphill Bicycle Race' by Alfred Jarry, from *Selected Works of Alfred Jarry*, ed. Roger Shaltuck and Simon Watson Taylor (Melhuen, 1965). Reprinted by permission of Methuen London.

This Fish is Loaded was compiled with considerable assistance from Atlas Press and from Alstair Brotchie, who was to have co-edited it but who was prevented by other commitments from doing so. The Editor acknowledges his contributions and suggestions with thanks, and recommends any reader with a taste for Surreal and bizarre literature to check out the publications of Atlas Press at Flat 5, Ormonde Mansions, 100 Southampton Row, London WC1.

INDEX